Elements of the
THEORY OF
PROBABILITY

WITHDRAW[

Elements of the
THEORY OF
PROBABILITY
by Émile Borel

Translated by John E. Freund
Professor of Mathematics, Arizona State University

• PRENTICE-HALL, INC. •
Englewood Cliffs, New Jersey

PRENTICE-HALL INTERNATIONAL, INC., *London*
PRENTICE-HALL OF AUSTRALIA, PTY., LTD., *Sydney*
PRENTICE-HALL OF CANADA, LTD., *Toronto*
PRENTICE-HALL OF INDIA (PRIVATE) LTD., *New Delhi*
PRENTICE-HALL OF JAPAN, INC., *Tokyo*

Originally published as

ÉLÉMENTS DE LA THÉORIE DES PROBABILITÉS *by Émile Borel*

Copyright 1950 by Albin Michel

Library of Congress Catalog Card Number: 65–15094

PRINTED IN THE UNITED STATES OF AMERICA. 27342—C

Author's Preface

In 1909 I published a book under the same title as this one; it had several editions but is no longer in print. Thus, I felt that the *Bibliothèque d'Éducation par la Science* should include a volume on the elements of probability. Although I had to introduce several new chapters to account for some new developments, the fundamental principles have become classical, having the same status as the elements of Euclidean geometry. Accordingly, some of the chapters were preserved with but minor modifications.

For half a century, the applications of the calculus of probability to the physical, biological, and social sciences have assumed an ever-increasing importance, and I have thus been led to publish (with several collaborators) a treatise on the calculus of probabilities and its applications. This treatise consists of 18 works, in 4 volumes, and it was necessary to supplement it with a series of monographs on probability which more or less cover the new developments of the theory. The present volume may be considered as an introduction to this treatise.

For those lacking the leisure to pursue the study of the theory of probability any further, this book should serve as a basis for understanding its most important applications.

I had to omit what might be called the philosophy of probability, namely, the relationship between this theory and the theory of knowledge. For those readers who might be interested in this subject, I would like to refer to my book *Le Hasard* and the last part of my treatise *Valeur Pratique et Philosophie des Probabilités*.

The elements of the theory of probability presented here should really constitute part of everyone's secondary education. Until such a reform has been accomplished, however, I hope that this volume will aid the faithful reader of the *Bibliothèque* in filling a serious gap in his general education.

ÉMILE BOREL

Translator's Preface

Although probability theory owes its early development to interest in games of chance, mathematicians as well as philosophers and scientists have become increasingly concerned with questions concerning the applicability of the theory to an ever-widening range of natural and social phenomena. This has raised questions about the meaning of "probability," questions about the interpretation of probability statements, and questions about the justifiability of the assumptions underlying various probabilistic models. Although there has been a recent upsurge in the teaching of probability on the secondary school and elementary college level, most of the attention has been devoted to the purely mathematical aspects of the theory (with special emphasis on the algebra of sets) and to straightforward applications to statistics. As a result, recent textbooks written essentially for the layman have ignored many of the fascinating problems related to probability theory which are of a philosophical rather than of a purely mathematical nature.

Even though the reader may disagree with some of the views expressed by the author—the translator does—he should find that the controversial aspects of probability shed an entirely new and fascinating light on the theory. It is of special interest to observe that in the author's opinion the material in this book (including questions of objective vs. subjective probabilities, questions of basing "rational" decisions on probabilities, questions concerning the appropriateness of equiprobability and other assumptions, questions concerning the probabilities of causes, and questions concerning other controversial matters) should be part of everyone's secondary education.

The problems in this book are numbered as in the French edition, with a few numbers missing. The only changes made in this translation were the substitution of some games of chance better known in the English-speaking world than the ones used by the author, and the omission of some footnote references to French works not readily available to most readers.

JOHN E. FREUND

Contents

PART ONE

Discrete Probabilities

CHAPTER ONE

The Game of Heads or Tails

1.1 *Definition of the Game*

A coin is tossed into the air and we bet on which side will be turned up after the toss; one of the sides is called "head" while the other is called "tail." This is the simplest problem of probability, if one adds the hypothesis that the chances for heads and tails are the same. So far as the equality of these chances is concerned, we shall omit all philosophical considerations and take it simply as an experimental fact or, if so desired, as the definition of the fact that the coin being used is "honest." Thus, it will be assumed from now on that the game is played with an honest coin. If the reader feels that a coin can never be completely "honest" owing to its irregular shape, one can substitute for it a symmetrical token which has been checked most rigorously by careful fabrication. Of course, such perfect symmetry can be only a limiting case, an abstract notion like the concept of a straight line, but it can be approximated sufficiently in practice, so that the conclusions to which it leads agree with experience.*

---

* Rigorously speaking, the absolute symmetry entails the indiscernibility of the two sides and, hence, the impossibility of the game. If the two sides differ in any respect, even if it is only in color, one can never be completely certain that such a difference does not have an effect. Nevertheless, it is possible to play with a perfectly symmetrical token, if one has motion pictures taken from various angles, which make it possible to follow, in slow motion, the movements of a face designated in advance. Also, we shall see later (in Chapter 6) how certain results of the calculus of probabilities can be subjected to experimental verification as rigorous as that of some of the results of the natural sciences.

1.2 *Some Simple Cases*

Let us first study the case where one plays a small number of games, and let us determine the outcomes that can be produced. The first game can result in either head or tail, which are equally likely—or as one usually says, each has a *probability* of *one in two*; we shall write this as 1:2 or as 0.5.* This result may be presented as follows:

Head   1:2

Tail   1:2

Regardless of the outcome of the first game, the second game must result in head or tail, and these two possibilities are again equally probable, since the outcome of the first game has no effect on that of the second. According to the famous statement by Joseph Bertrand, *a coin has neither conscience nor memory*. It is important to stress this point, in spite of its self-evidence, for if it is not understood perfectly, without restriction or reservation, it is useless to pursue the study of the theory of probability.

It is mainly the practice of gambling which sets certain stubborn minds against this notion of the independence of successive events. They observe that heads and tails appear about equally often in a long series of tosses, and they conclude that if there has been a long run of tails, it should be followed by a head; they look at this as a *debt* owed to them by the game.† A little reflection will suffice, however, to convince anyone of the childishness of this anthropomorphism. The reasons according to which the chances for head and tail are equal subsist for each game, and one cannot conceive of a mechanism through which the results of previous games can possibly modify the equality of chances. The anthropomorphic belief in the memory and the conscience of a coin has no positive foundation. Of course, this would not suffice to condemn the notion, unless one finds other means to account for the observation that heads and tails appear in about equal numbers in many games. Later we shall see how one can arrive at the most satisfactory explanation of such empirical results, precisely, by assuming the independence of successive games; all pretexts to contest this assumption of independence will thus disappear.

Let us return to the second game. Combining the outcomes to which it can lead with the results obtained in the first game, we get the following table:

---

* A rigorous definition of probability will be given in the next chapter; this empirical definition will suffice for the moment.

† This observation applies also to the red or black in roulette, or to the banker's winning or losing in Baccara, etc. Such games are more complex than Heads or Tails, but they have numerous analogies with this simpler game.

```
        H
    H <
        T
        H
    T <
        T
```

where H and T stand, respectively, for head and tail, the first column corresponds to the outcome of the first game, and the second column corresponds to the outcome of the second game. We find that the combination of the two games leads to four equiprobable outcomes. Each outcome has a probability of *one in four*, that is, 1:4 or 0.25, and they can also be presented as follows:

$$
\begin{array}{ll}
\text{H H} & 1{:}4 \\
\text{H T} & 1{:}4 \\
\text{T H} & 1{:}4 \\
\text{T T} & 1{:}4
\end{array}
\left.\begin{array}{l} \\ \end{array}\right\} 2{:}4 = 1{:}2
$$

We have combined the two outcomes HT and TH since they have the common property that each contains one head and one tail; *they are identical if one does not consider the order in which the H's and T's are obtained.* From this point of view only three outcomes are possible: both games result in heads, only one game results in heads, or neither game results in heads. In other words, if a player bets on heads, he can win either zero, one, or two times. The respective probabilities of these eventualities are not equal, as a total lack of reflection might have led us to believe. The case where the player wins once in the two games consists of the two combinations HT and TH, and its probability is thus *one-half*; each of the two other cases has a probability of *one-fourth*.

Considering a third game, we find that analogous reasoning leads to the following table:

```
                H
            H <
                T
        H <
                H
            T <
                T
                H
            H <
                T
        T <
                H
            T <
                T
```

where the first column corresponds to the first game, the second column to the second game, and the third column to the third game. One finds that there are all in all 8 equiprobable combinations. Modifying the order of the

above table by interchanging the middle outcomes (and thus bringing together all combinations leading to the same general results), we get the
following table:

$$
\begin{array}{lll}
\text{H H H} & 1:8 & \\
\text{H H T} & 1:8 \\
\text{H T H} & 1:8 \Big\} 3:8 \\
\text{T H H} & 1:8 \\
\text{H T T} & 1:8 \\
\text{T H T} & 1:8 \Big\} 3:8 \\
\text{T T H} & 1:8 \\
\text{T T T} & 1:8 &
\end{array}
$$

It can be seen that the player who bets on heads, for example, has 1 chance
in 8 of winning three games, 3 chances in 8 of winning two games, 3 chances
in 8 of winning one game, and 1 chance in 8 of winning none.

In the same way one could construct analogous tables for four games.
We shall give only the second of these two tables, namely,

$$
\begin{array}{lll}
\text{H H H H} & 1:16 & \\
\text{H H H T} & 1:16 \\
\text{H H T H} & 1:16 \\
\text{H T H H} & 1:16 \Big\} 4:16 = 1:4 \\
\text{T H H H} & 1:16 \\
\text{H H T T} & 1:16 \\
\text{H T H T} & 1:16 \\
\text{H T T H} & 1:16 \\
\text{T H H T} & 1:16 \Big\} 6:16 = 3:8 \\
\text{T H T H} & 1:16 \\
\text{T T H H} & 1:16 \\
\text{H T T T} & 1:16 \\
\text{T H T T} & 1:16 \\
\text{T T H T} & 1:16 \Big\} 4:16 = 1:4 \\
\text{T T T H} & 1:16 \\
\text{T T T T} & 1:16 &
\end{array}
$$

It can be seen that the player who bets on heads has 1 chance in 16 of
winning four games, 4 chances in 16 (or 1 chance in 4) of winning three, 6
chances in 16 (or 3 chances in 8) of winning two, 4 chances in 16 (or 1 chance
in 4) of winning one, and 1 chance in 16 of winning none.

1.3 *Some Remarks*

Without going into further detail, one can see the simple mechanism by
which one obtains unequal probabilities for the various total results in a
series of games, even though equal probabilities are assumed for the two
outcomes in each game. For example, for 4 games there are 6 combinations

consisting of 2 heads and 2 tails. Taken individually, each of these combinations is no more probable than the one consisting of 4 heads; however, if one considers them as a whole, there are 6 times as many chances of obtaining one of these combinations, not designated in advance, as there are for obtaining 4 heads. If two players play a large number of series of 4 games of heads and tails, they will discover without difficulty that the most frequent case is the one where each player wins two games. This case should occur on the average 6 times in 16.* The case where one player wins three games should occur 4 times in 16 for each player (and, hence, 8 times in 16, if one does not specify which of the two players wins the three games). It follows that this case occurs more frequently than the case where each player wins the same number of games. Finally, it will happen only 1 time in 16 that a specified player will win all four games (and, hence, 2 times in 16 that all four games will be won by one of the two players).

It would be a grave error to conclude from these statements that the combination HHHT, for example, is more probable than the combination HHHH: namely, that the fourth game has the peculiar tendency to yield a tail when the first three games have yielded heads. If the combinations yielding 3 heads are more probable than the combination yielding 4 heads, this is not because each of them is more probable; it is because they are more numerous. There are four such combinations, since the game whose outcome is tails can be either the first, the second, the third, or the fourth. Only the last of these four cases can occur when the first three games have yielded heads.

1.4 Pascal's Triangle

If one considers a large number of successive games of heads or tails, it is easy to give a rule for the probability of obtaining m heads in n games. It is apparent that the total number of possible outcomes is 2^n and that each of the outcomes has the same probability; corresponding to each possible combination for the first $n - 1$ games there are 2 combinations for all n games, since the nth game can yield either head or tail. It was in this manner that we obtained 2 combinations for one game, 4 combinations for two games, 8 for three games, and so on.

How many of the 2^n combinations contain exactly m heads? Denoting this number by C_n^m, let us point out that in order to obtain m heads it is necessary that either the first $n - 1$ games yield m heads and the nth yields tails, or the first $n - 1$ games yield $m - 1$ heads and the nth yields heads. The first alternative furnishes those combinations where there are m heads

---

* We are anticipating here the results of Chapter 4, but it should be observed that the assertion is made in the light of the example, and that it does not entail any circular reasoning.

in $n - 1$ games; that is, it furnished C_{n-1}^m combinations. Similarly, the second alternative furnishes C_{n-1}^{m-1} combinations, and it follows that

$$C_n^m = C_{n-1}^{m-1} + C_{n-1}^m$$

One thus arrives at the following rule, which leads to Pascal's triangle: *In the first row one writes twice the number 1; then one obtains each other number by adding the number immediately above to the number to the left of the one immediately above. In the application of this rule it is assumed mentally that the lines are extended by zeros to the left and to the right.* One thus obtains the following table:

1	1								
1	2	1							
1	3	3	1						
1	4	6	4	1					
1	5	10	10	5	1				
1	6	15	20	15	6	1			
1	7	21	35	35	21	7	1		
1	8	28	56	70	56	28	8	1	
1	9	36	84	126	126	84	36	9	1
1	10	45	120	210	252	210	120	45	10	1

This table can easily be continued, and it is of great importance in the solution of simple problems of probability. The first four rows contain the numbers we obtained in Section 1.2 for 1, 2, 3, and 4 games; the fifth row is obtained by the following calculations: $0 + 1 = 1$, $1 + 4 = 5$, $4 + 6 = 10$, $6 + 4 = 10$, $4 + 1 = 5$, and $1 + 0 = 1$.

By virtue of these calculations, the sum of the numbers in the fifth row is twice that of the numbers in the fourth row; evidently, it is equal to $2 \cdot 16 = 32$. There are thus 32 possible combinations for 5 games, among which 1 contains 5 heads, 5 contain exactly 4 heads, 10 contain exactly 3 heads, 10 contain exactly 2 heads, 5 contain only 1 head, and 1 contains no heads.

It should be noted that the various rows of the table are symmetrical; that is, numbers equidistant from the two extremes of a row are equal. In rows corresponding to an even number of games the numbers increase towards the middle, and the greatest number corresponds to an even distribution between heads and tails. In rows corresponding to an odd number of games there are two equal numbers in the middle; they are larger than the other numbers in the row and they correspond to the two cases where there is one more head than tail or one more tail than head.

1.5 *Some Elementary Problems*

PROBLEM 1. *Playing heads or tails, does a player have a greater chance of winning 3 games in 4 or 5 games in 8?* This question must be formulated more precisely by indicating whether the player must win exactly 3 games in

4, or whether he must win *at least* 3 games in 4. In other words, if the player wins 4 games, is this to be included among the cases where he wins 3? Evidently, this is only a matter of convention and we shall examine both cases.

First case: the statement is taken in the strict sense, namely, the number of games won must be exactly 3 in 4. Referring to Pascal's triangle, it can be seen that there are 4 favorable cases out of 16 where the player wins 3 games in 4, and that there are 56 favorable cases out of 256 where the player wins 5 games in 8. Thus, for winning 3 games in 4 the probability is 4/16 = 1/4, and for winning 5 games in 8 it is 56/256 = 7/32. It follows that it is more advantageous to bet on winning 3 games in 4 than on winning 5 games in 8.

Second case: the statement is taken in its wider sense, namely, the number of games won must be at least 3 and 5. Pascal's triangle shows that the number of favorable cases for winning 4 or 3 games in 4 is 1 + 4 = 5, and that the number of favorable cases for winning 8, 7, 6, or 5 games in 8 is 1 + 8 + 28 + 56 = 93. Thus, the probability of winning at least 3 games in 4 is 5/16 = 80/256, and the probability of winning at least 5 games in 8 is 93/256. It follows that it is more advantageous to bet on winning at least 5 games in 8 than on winning at least 3 games in 4.

PROBLEM 2. *Is it more advantageous to bet on winning at least 5 games in 7 than on winning at least 6 games in 9?* For the first alternative the number of favorable cases is 1 + 7 + 21 = 29 out of a total of 128 possibilities, and the probability of winning at least 5 games in 7 is 29/128 = 1/4 − 3/128. For the second alternative the number of favorable cases is 1 + 9 + 36 + 84 = 130 out of a total of 512 possibilities, and the probability of winning at least 6 games in 9 is 130/512 = 1/4 + 1/256. The second value is higher, and it follows that the second alternative is more advantageous.

There is nothing to be gained by giving further examples of such simple problems; in order to treat somewhat more complicated cases, it will be convenient to introduce first the concept of mathematical expectation.

1.6 *Mathematical Expectation*

When one talks about the *mathematical expectation* of a player, one refers to the product of his possible gains and the probability that they will be realized. Let us first consider the case where the possible gain is unique. For example, if Peter plays heads or tails and he receives $100 when the coin comes up heads, the probability that he will win this amount is 0.5 and his mathematical expectation is $50. If Paul receives $1,000 when two games of heads or tails yield two heads, his mathematical expectation is 1,000(0.25) = $250.

It can be seen that the expression *mathematical expectation* must be regarded as a special term having a well-defined meaning; one cannot look for its meaning by referring to the usual meaning of each of the two terms *expectation* and *mathematical*. In the ordinary sense of the word, Paul has a certain expectation of obtaining $1,000. If this expectation is not realized he receives nothing at all, and in any case he will never receive $250, the amount of his mathematical expectation. In spite of this, there are certain advantages to preserving the expression mathematical expectation, even though it is consecrated by usage; there is seldom any real advantage in introducing new terms.

A game is said to be *equitable* if the mathematical expectation of each player is equal to his stake. A mathematical expectation of a certain amount may thus be traded against this amount, *if one can find a player disposed to play an appropriate equitable game*. For example, if I were to receive $2 in the case where a game of heads or tails yields head, my mathematical expectation is $1 and it can be sold at this price to a player disposed to take my place. In this particular example it should be easy to sell the mathematical expectation, but this would not be the case if the stake in a game of heads or tails were $100,000,000. Sometimes the commercial value of a mathematical expectation exceeds its numerical value; this is because of the public's taste for lotteries and the restrictions imposed on them by law. It is easy to sell for a dollar a lottery ticket with a mathematical expectation of 30 cents.*

The following illustrates the great advantage of the concept of mathematical expectation: whereas the combination of various probabilities can entail complicated calculations, the rule for mathematical expectations is simple and intuitive: *to obtain the mathematical expectation connected with several events one has only to take the sum of their respective mathematical expectations*.

To illustrate, suppose that Paul is to play three games of heads or tails; if he wins the first game he will receive $10, if he wins the second game he will receive $20, and if he wins the third game he will receive $40. His mathematical expectation is $5 + 10 + 20 = \$35$, and this is the sum for which he might sell his chances to a player disposed to playing an honest game. In case this is not immediately apparent, it should suffice to observe that if a single buyer were to purchase Paul's mathematical expectation as well as that of his opponent, he should pay both of them the same amount (since their situations are supposedly identical); since the buyer is assured to receive $70 no matter what happens, he should pay each opponent $35. In that case the game would assure him neither a certain gain nor a certain loss.

It will be accepted as evident that if a match is composed of several successive games and each game is equitable, then the whole match is equitable. This principle is of great value in the solution of certain problems.

---

* To obtain the mathematical expectation of a lottery ticket one has only to divide the sum of the prizes by the number of tickets. This would be the value of the ticket if the promoter of the lottery were to make no profit and incur no expenses.

1.7 *Problems on Mathematical Expectation*

PROBLEM 3. *Three players, A, B, and C, play heads or tails under the following conditions: A and B play the first game, after which the loser retires and his place is taken by C; this is repeated after each game, the loser retires and his place is taken by the third player. The player who first wins two consecutive games receives m dollars. What is the mathematical expectation of each player (1) after the first game, and (2) before the first game?* Let us suppose that A wins the first game and let us designate by a, b, and c the mathematical expectations of A, B, and C after the first game; they are, respectively, the player who remains, the player who retires, and the player who enters the game. If A wins the second game, the game will be finished and A will be the winner; if A loses the second game he will become the player who retires, B will become the one who enters, and C will become the one who remains. In the first case (A wins) A receives m dollars while B and C receive nothing; in the second case (A loses) the mathematical expectation of A becomes b, that of B becomes c, and that of C becomes a. Writing the mathematical expectation of each player as the sum of the mathematical expectations resulting from the two cases and putting the probability for each case equal to 1/2, we obtain

$$a = \frac{m}{2} + \frac{b}{2}$$

$$b = 0 + \frac{c}{2}$$

$$c = 0 + \frac{a}{2}$$

The solution of these equations is given by

$$a = \frac{4}{7}m, \qquad b = \frac{1}{7}m, \qquad c = \frac{2}{7}m$$

These are the mathematical expectations after the first game. To obtain the mathematical expectations of the players before the first game, a', b', and c', it suffices to observe that the mathematical expectation of C is not affected by the outcome of the first game. The *sum* of the mathematical expectations of A and B is not affected either, for if someone were to buy A and B's chances, it would not matter to him whether the first game is won by A or B. Finally, one has $a' = b'$ and it follows that

$$a' = b' = \frac{a+b}{2} = \frac{5}{14}m, \qquad c' = c = \frac{2}{7}m = \frac{4}{14}m$$

It can be seen that before the game starts the position of players A and B is a little better than that of player C. If $m = 14$ dollars, the mathematical expectations of A and B are each worth $5, while that of C is worth only $4.

We shall return to this problem, sometimes called the *problem of the pool*, to study it further with the aid of certain theorems of probability.

PROBLEM 4. *Paul plays n games of heads or tails and he is to receive a dollars each time that three consecutive games contain two heads, and b dollars each time there are three heads in a row. What is his mathematical expectation?* To solve this problem one has only to observe that there are $n - 2$ sets of three successive games beginning with the first, the second, . . . , and the $(n - 2)$nd. For each of these sets the mathematical expectation is

$$\frac{3a}{8} + \frac{b}{8}$$

because there are 3 chances in 8 of winning a dollars and 1 chance in 8 of winning b dollars. The total mathematical expectation is thus

$$\frac{(n - 2)(3a + b)}{8}$$

More complicated problems of this kind will be given later.

1.8 *General Formulas for n Games*

When the number of games of heads or tails is large, Pascal's triangle ceases to be of much use, and it is preferable to refer directly to a formula furnishing the number of combinations containing q heads in n games. Combinatorial analysis, which includes Pascal's triangle, tells us that this number is given by the formula*

$$C_n^q = \frac{n(n - 1) \cdot \ldots \cdot (n - q + 1)}{1 \cdot 2 \cdot \ldots \cdot q} = \frac{n!}{q!(n - q)!}$$

It is easy to prove this formula by direct means. If in one of the combinations where n games contain q heads we replace one of the heads by a tail, we obtain one of the combinations where n games contain $q - 1$ heads. Since this substitution can be made in q different ways for each of the C_n^q combinations, we obtain altogether $q \cdot C_n^q$ combinations containing $q - 1$ heads and $n - q + 1$ tails. Moreover it is clear that each of the C_n^{q-1} combinations containing $q - 1$ heads and $n - q + 1$ tails is thus obtained $n - q + 1$ times, since, by replacing one of the $n - q + 1$ tails by a head in one of these combinations, one returns to one of the original combinations by inverse substitution. One has thus

$$q \cdot C_n^q = (n - q + 1)C_n^{q-1}$$

or
$$C_n^q = \frac{n - q + 1}{q} \cdot C_n^{q-1}$$

---

* As is customary, $n! = 1 \cdot 2 \cdot \ldots \cdot n$, and it is called n *factorial*.

Similarly, one has

$$C_n^{q-1} = \frac{n-q+2}{q-1} \cdot C_n^{q-2}$$

$$C_n^{q-2} = \frac{n-q+3}{q-2} \cdot C_n^{q-3}$$

$$\cdots\cdots\cdots\cdots\cdots\cdots$$

$$C_n^2 = \frac{n-1}{2} \cdot C_n^1$$

$$C_n^1 = n$$

The last equation expresses the fact that the single head can be in the first game, the second game, ..., or in the last game, and this gives n possible combinations. Multiplying the respective sides of all these equations, one finally obtains the formula for C_n^q given above.

It should also be noted that if one considers the product $(H + T)^n = (H + T)(H + T) \cdot \ldots \cdot (H + T)$ and if one multiplies out the product on the right-hand side, taking care to preserve the order of the factors in each partial product, one obtains 2^n terms corresponding precisely to all possible combinations of n letters which are either H or T. If one then combines similar terms, it is clear that the coefficient of $H^q T^{n-q}$ equals C_n^q, the number of combinations containing q letters H. One thus obtains the binomial formula of Newton, namely,

$$(H + T)^n = H^n + C_n^1 H^{n-1}T + \ldots + C_n^q H^{n-q}T^q + \ldots + T^n$$

making use of the fact that $C_n^q = C_n^{n-q}$. The quantities C_n^q are usually referred to as *binomial coefficients*, and they play an important role in many problems of probability.

It should also be noted that, as a result of the preceding considerations, one has

$$1 + C_n^1 + C_n^2 + \ldots + C_n^q + \ldots + C_n^{n-1} + 1 = 2^n$$

since the total number of all possible combinations is 2^n. This result may also be obtained by expanding $(1 + 1)^n$ by means of the binomial formula of Newton.

In Sections 3.2 and 3.4 we shall give formulas for obtaining approximations of $n!$ and, hence, approximations of the coefficients C_n^q. These approximation formulas are all the more useful when n is very large. When n does not exceed 30, it is preferable to use a table giving the values of $\log n!$; such a table may be found in most tables of logarithms.

1.9 *Certain Paradoxes*

We could end here our exposition of the essential principles of the theory of "Heads or Tails." Once these principles are established, all consequences are deduced by purely logical reasoning; assertions contrary to these consequences must be considered as incorrect, without even examining the arguments on which they are supposed to be based. This approach would conform with the spirit of mathematics. However, we shall not take this approach, since everyone does not have a mathematical mind; furthermore, many excellent minds seem to have an aversion to logical reasoning so far as questions of probability are concerned. Although it is desirable to have the principles of probability accepted by as many people as possible, it is worthwhile to devote some lines to arguments that might arise. Of course, from a purely mathematical point of view such discussions are useless.

The following is one of the main sources of the paradoxical reasoning to which we shall return in Section 3.3: *if an event is extremely probable, one has the tendency to accept its realization without question.* There is an error here which is undoubtedly very small, but the accumulation of such errors can lead to completely incorrect results. Later on we shall study the mechanics of such an accumulation of errors; for the moment we shall merely demonstrate the absurdity to which one can be led by this kind of thinking.

Suppose that one plays a great number of games of heads or tails and that one records the results. Assuming that the stake is the same for each game, one would thus always know the winnings or losses of a player betting on heads. If one actually played such a series of games, one would note that after a certain number of games, usually few, rarely more than 100, and hardly ever more than 1,000, the winnings and losses are reduced to zero. After that, the next game will yield a loss or a gain, and if it is a gain, we shall refer to the entire series of games as "favorable." If the next game had yielded a loss, we would have continued the game until the next return to zero, and there would then have been one chance in two of obtaining a "favorable" series ending in the subsequent game. This process is continued until a favorable series is obtained. Practically speaking, experience would show the reader who may want to perform this experiment that a favorable series is usually obtained after a relatively small number of games, and that such a series would *surely* be obtained if one had the patience to play, if necessary, some thousands of games.*

Suppose now that Peter and Paul play heads or tails and that the game is continued until Paul realizes a favorable series.† Thus, Paul's winnings are equal to his stake. This ends the game, but it is continued on the next day with Paul playing against John; again they play until Paul realizes a favorable series. Continuing in this way, Paul could regularly win an amount

---

* The word "surely" is italicized, because it is here that the error is introduced. We should have said "practically certain," implying that the probability of its not occurring is extremely small (see also Section 3.3). In other words, one would not run into trouble more than once in a hundred years if one played one game per second and recorded the results. Nevertheless, it is not a mathematical certainty.

† If Paul wins the first game, this game by itself constitutes a favorable series.

equal to his stake. If we now suppose that Paul plays against the same opponent Peter an indefinite number of games, Paul could, without waiting until the next day, consider the game as interrupted after each favorable series and start recording again from that moment on. Since nothing distinguishes one moment from another and since one can always suppose that the game begins at some arbitrary instant, it follows that Paul will have an unlimited number of favorable series and, hence, an unlimited gain. This would be true, at least, if there were no limit to the duration of the game and to the duration of human life.

Referring to the identical series of games, Peter could reason in the same way, and it follows that his gain is also unlimited, provided the game is played for a sufficient length of time. We have thus arrived at the absurd result that each player will realize a gain which increases with time. Clearly, this contradicts the original argument according to which some thousands of games would suffice to reestablish the balance between the two players. Let us be satisfied, for the moment, with having put the reader on guard against the drawbacks of a certain kind of reasoning. We shall study this question in more detail after we have acquired the necessary theory.

CHAPTER TWO

Definitions and Theorems

2.1 *The Definition of Probability*

It is customary to define probability as *the ratio of the number of favorable cases to the total number of cases, provided that all cases may be regarded as equally probable.* This definition gives the impression of a vicious circle; after all, how can one know whether all cases are equally probable when one does not know their probabilities? Actually, there is no vicious circle in assuming that one has a primitive notion about the meaning of "equally probable" when one defines the mathematically precise meaning of the word "probability." Logicians who pretend to construct logical systems without vicious circles forget that it is impossible not to use ordinary language. This is true not only in the definition of scientific terms; ordinary language must be looked upon as a universal acquisition of each individual, an acquisition which presupposes many vicious circles.

Thus, it is natural to inquire under what conditions one can regard various possible events as equally probable. The best answer to this question is to give a few examples. If one rolls a die having the shape of a cube and consisting of a homogeneous substance, it is reasonable to regard its six faces as equiprobable. If an urn contains a number of balls having the same shape and consisting of the same substance, and if one draws one ball after they have been thoroughly mixed, the drawing of any one ball is as likely as that of any other ball. The situation is somewhat more complicated when the equality of probabilities is postulated by definition or when it is regarded as an experimental result. This question is important so far as applications are concerned, but it is without interest from a purely mathematical point of view and we shall not pursue it further.

16

2.2 *Fundamental Properties of Probability*

Let us designate by N the total number of possible cases, supposedly all equally probable, and by n the number of favorable cases. Thus, the probability p is given by the formula

$$p = \frac{n}{N}$$

and it can be seen that it is *always a fraction less than or equal to 1*. It equals 1 only when $n = N$, namely, when all cases are favorable and the probability is transformed into *certainty*.

Besides the probability of a given event one must often consider the probability of the corresponding unfavorable event (supposing, for the moment, that all events other than the favorable event are grouped under this heading). For example, if an urn contains N balls among which n are white while the others are red, black, etc., and if one considers the drawing of a white ball as a favorable event, then the drawing of a ball which is not white is an unfavorable event. Designating the probability of an unfavorable event by q, we have

$$q = \frac{N - n}{N} = 1 - \frac{n}{N} = 1 - p$$

since $N - n$ of the balls are not white and, hence, the number of favorable cases for this contrary event is $N - n$. The result we have obtained may be written as

$$p + q = 1$$

that is to say, *the sum of the probabilities of a favorable event and the corresponding unfavorable event is equal to unity*. It is important to remember that by "unfavorable events" one understands all those which are not favorable, without distinguishing between various alternatives. Thus, if someone is concerned with winning a game of chess, the unfavorable cases include all those where he does not win; that is, they include losses as well as tie games.

If an event is very probable, its probability p is very close to 1, and the probability q is, therefore, very close to 0. In everyday language one sometimes says that a probability is very large. This does not agree with the mathematical definition according to which p cannot exceed 1; instead of saying that a probability is *very large*, one should say that it is *close to 1*. The habit of referring to such a probability as large owes its origin to the fact that one really compares the probability of the favorable event with that of the unfavorable event. If the first of these probabilities is much larger than the other, one says that p is very large, although what is large is really the *ratio* of the two probabilities. This ratio might be called the *relative probability* of the two events, in which case the probability defined above could be called the *absolute probability*. Nevertheless, we shall not emphasize this distinction and shall refer to absolute probabilities simply as probabilities, since they are the ones which most frequently arise in practice. There is no advantage in unnecessarily complicating one's language, although it is well to be aware that in everyday language one often uses the word probability in the sense of a relative probability, that is, one thinks of the ratio R defined by the formula

$$R = \frac{p}{q} = \frac{p}{1-p} = \frac{n}{N-n}$$

For example, if an urn contains 999 white balls and 1 black ball, and if one considers the drawing of a white ball as a favorable event, then $p = 0.999$, $q = 0.001$, and $R = 999$. The probability p of a favorable event is very close to 1, and the relative probability R is very large.

If several mutually exclusive events exhaust all possibilities, the sum of their probabilities is equal to 1. Suppose, for example, that an urn contains N identical balls and that each is inscribed with one of the numbers $1, 2, \ldots,$ or m. If n_1 is the number of balls inscribed with the number 1, n_2 is the number of balls inscribed with the number 2, and so forth, the probability p_1 of drawing a ball inscribed with the number 1 is evidently

$$p_1 = \frac{n_1}{N}$$

Similarly,

$$p_2 = \frac{n_2}{N}, \ldots, p_m = \frac{n_m}{N}$$

and it follows that

$$p_1 + p_2 + \ldots + p_m = \frac{n_1 + n_2 + \ldots + n_m}{N} = 1$$

since $n_1 + n_2 + \ldots + n_m = N$.

2.3 Total Probabilities

Let us consider an urn containing N balls of which a are red, b are white, and the others are neither red nor white. The probability of drawing a red ball is $\alpha = a/N$ and the probability of drawing a white ball is $\beta = b/N$. The probability p of drawing a ball that is either red or white is evidently

$$p = \frac{a+b}{N}$$

and one immediately notices the relation $p = \alpha + \beta$, which expresses the *theorem of total probabilities*. To formulate this theorem it is important to state precisely under what conditions the above result has been obtained. The favorable event (whose probability we wanted to find) was the drawing of a red ball or a white ball; this favorable event could occur in two ways which are mutually exclusive (if the ball drawn is red it cannot be white, and vice versa). The probabilities corresponding to the two possibilities are α and β, and the desired probability p is equal to their sum. It is obvious that the reasoning would have been identical in the case where there are more than two ways of obtaining a favorable event; for example, if one considered as favorable the drawing of a red, white, green, purple, or yellow ball, while all other colors were excluded. We can thus state the following theorem of total probabilities:

THEOREM. *If an event can occur in several different ways which are mutually exclusive, its probability equals the sum of the probabilities corresponding to the different alternatives.*

In the application of this theorem it is always important to verify that the alternatives are, in fact, mutually exclusive. Consider, for example, the following problem:

PROBLEM 5. *Peter and Paul play heads or tails under the following conditions: if the first game yields heads Peter wins; if not, they play two more games and Peter wins if at least two of the three games yield heads. What is the probability that Peter will win?*

One might reason as follows: Peter can win in two different ways, by winning the first game or by winning at least two out of three. Each of these alternatives has a probability of 1/2, and one might thus be led to conclude that the total probability is 1, that is, certainty. This is obviously absurd: if one considers a set of three games of heads or tails, it is true that the probability of obtaining at least two heads is 1/2, since there are four favorable outcomes HHT, HTH, THH, and HHH among the eight possibilities. However, among these four combinations there are three where the first game yields heads, and in that case Peter wins without having to play the other games. These possibilities of winning are, therefore, excluded by the first alternative. Moreover, it would be incorrect to reason that there is but 1 chance in 4 of obtaining THH and, hence, that the probability for the second alternative is 1/4, once the four cases where the first game yields heads are excluded. What one must do is to multiply the probability for the second alternative (2 heads in 3 games) by the probability that the first game will not yield heads. Then one adds this result to the probability that the first game yields heads, and one obtains $\frac{1}{2} + \frac{1}{2} \cdot \frac{1}{4} = \frac{5}{8}$.

2.4 *Composite Probabilities*

Let us consider two urns; the first contains N balls of which a are white, and the second contains N' balls of which a' are white. Thus, the probability of drawing a white ball from the first urn is $\alpha = a/N$, and the probability of drawing a white ball from the second urn is $\beta = a'/N'$. Suppose now that one draws one ball from each urn and that one wants to find the probability p that both balls are white. To begin with, let us determine the total number of possible cases, and let us assume for this purpose that the balls in the first urn are numbered from 1 to N while those in the second urn are numbered from $1'$ to N'. Now, the drawing may consist of ball 1 from the first urn and any one of the N' balls from the second; this gives N' possibilities, all equally probable. The drawing may also consist of ball 2 from the first urn and any one of the N' balls from the second; this gives another N' possibilities, equally probable among themselves and having the same probability as each of the first N' possibilities. Thus, there are N' possibilities corresponding to each of the N balls in the first urn, and there are altogether $N \cdot N'$ possibilities.* The number of favorable cases may be counted in the same way: for each of the a white balls in the first urn there are a' favorable possibilities corresponding, respectively, to the a' white balls in the second urn. Thus, there are $a \cdot a'$ favorable cases and the probability p is given by the formula

$$p = \frac{a \cdot a'}{N \cdot N'}$$

It can be seen that one has $p = \alpha \cdot \beta$ and this formula expresses the *theorem of composite probabilities*. Before we state this theorem in words, let us generalize the conditions under which it was obtained. Suppose we have three urns, of which one will be called the first urn, while the other two, painted white and black, will be called the *second white urn* and the *second black urn*. First one draws a ball from the first urn; if it is white one draws the second ball from the *second white urn*, and if it is not white one draws the second ball from the *second black urn*. What is the probability of obtaining two white balls? Clearly, if α is the probability of drawing a white ball from the first urn and β is the probability of drawing a white ball from the second *white* urn, one has again $p = \alpha \cdot \beta$. Note that one needs the second *black* urn only when the first drawing does not yield a white ball, in which

---

* In the case where $N = 6$ and the N balls are numbered 0, 1, 2, 3, 4, 5, and $N' = 10$ and the N' balls are numbered 0, 1, 2, 3, 4, 5, 6, 7, 8, 9, the results of the drawings may be presented as in the following table, where the first number is the one drawn from the first urn and the second number is the one drawn from the second urn:

00	01	02	03	04	05	06	07	08	09
10	11	12	13	14	15	16	17	18	19
20	21	22	23	24	25	26	27	28	29
30	31	32	33	34	35	36	37	38	39
40	41	42	43	44	45	46	47	48	49
50	51	52	53	54	55	56	57	58	59

As can be seen, there are altogether 60 possibilities.

case one certainly does not have a favorable case and the second drawing is irrelevant. Thus, the probability of a favorable case would not be affected if the second black urn were replaced by one having a completely arbitrary composition, say, that of the second white urn. The problem is thus reduced to the case already treated, but it will nevertheless permit a somewhat more general formulation.

THEOREM. *If an event consists of the successive occurrence of two events, its probability equals the product of the probability of the first event and the probability of the second event, given that the first event has occurred. More generally, the probability for the occurrence of several successive events is obtained by multiplying the probabilities of the individual events, assuming in each case that all preceding events have occurred.*

Limiting ourselves to the case of two events, it is clear that the last restriction is unnecessary if the probability of the occurrence of the second event is the same regardless of whether or not the first event has occurred. If that is the case, one considers the two events as *independent*.

Let us give an example to illustrate the error one can make by not taking into account whether the first event has occurred.

PROBLEM 6. *An urn contains 90 balls numbered from 1 to 90. What is the probability that the number on a ball drawn from this urn is divisible by 6 as well as by 10?* Evidently, there is 1 chance in 6 that the number is divisible by 6 and 1 chance in 10 that it is divisible by 10. The respective probabilities are thus 1/6 and 1/10, but it would be wrong to conclude that the composite probability is 1/60. If a number is divisible by 6 it is also divisible by 2; hence, to have the number divisible by 10 it is sufficient to add the condition that it must be divisible by 5. The probability that the number is divisible by 10, given that it is divisible by 6, is thus 1/5, and it follows that the correct value of the composite probability is $\frac{1}{6} \cdot \frac{1}{5} = \frac{1}{30}$. This result can easily be obtained directly: if a number is to be divisible by 6 and 10, it is necessary and sufficient that it is divisible by 30; hence, the probability is 1/30.*

2.5 *Applications to Successive Drawings from an Urn*

PROBLEM 7. *An urn contains N balls, of which a are white. If three balls are drawn in succession, what is the probability that they are all white?* To apply the rule for composite probabilities let us observe that the probability for the first ball is a/N; then there are $N - 1$ balls left among which

---

* It should be noted that these calculations are correct because 90 is divisible by 30. The probability that a number less than or equal to $Ma + r$, where r is less than a, is divisible by a equals $\dfrac{M}{Ma + r}$; it reduces to $1/a$ for $r = 0$, and it is very close to $1/a$ when M is large, regardless of the value given to $r < a$.

$a - 1$ are white, and the probability for the second drawing is $\dfrac{a - 1}{N - 1}$; after that there are $N - 2$ balls left in the urn of which $a - 2$ are white, and the probability for the third drawing is $\dfrac{a - 2}{N - 2}$. It follows that the required composite probability is

$$\frac{a}{N} \cdot \frac{a - 1}{N - 1} \cdot \frac{a - 2}{N - 2} = \frac{a(a - 1)(a - 2)}{N(N - 1)(N - 2)}$$

For example, if a deck of 32 cards contains 4 kings, the probability of drawing 3 kings in a row is obtained by substituting $N = 32$ and $a = 4$; it is equal to

$$\frac{4 \cdot 3 \cdot 2}{32 \cdot 31 \cdot 30} = \frac{1}{4 \cdot 31 \cdot 10} = \frac{1}{1,240}$$

that is, one has one chance in 1,240.

Similarly, if a deck of 52 playing cards contains 13 clubs, the probability of obtaining 3 clubs in 3 drawings is

$$\frac{13 \cdot 12 \cdot 11}{52 \cdot 51 \cdot 50} = \frac{11}{17 \cdot 50} = \frac{11}{850}$$

One has slightly better than 1 chance in 78. With a deck of 32 cards the analogous probability would be

$$\frac{8 \cdot 7 \cdot 6}{32 \cdot 31 \cdot 30} = \frac{7}{4 \cdot 31 \cdot 5} = \frac{7}{620}$$

and one would have less than 1 chance in 88. We have shown the details of the calculations, which are simplified by the cancellation of common factors.

PROBLEM 8. *If an urn contains N balls of which a are white and the others are black, what is the probability of obtaining one white ball and one black ball in two successive drawings from the urn?* One can treat this problem by combining the theorems for total and composite probabilities. The desired event may be produced either by first drawing a white ball and then drawing a black ball, or by first drawing a black ball and then drawing a white ball. It is thus a total probability and its value is

$$\frac{a}{N} \cdot \frac{N - a}{N - 1} + \frac{N - a}{N} \cdot \frac{a}{N - 1} = \frac{2a(N - a)}{N(N - 1)}$$

This result was easily obtained due to the simplicity of the problem. In general, it is preferable to enumerate all possible cases by the methods of combinatorial analysis, as in the following example.

PROBLEM 9. *An urn contains 32 balls of which 8 are white, 8 are red, 8 are black, and 8 are blue. First one ball is drawn and its color is observed. Then*

5 more balls are drawn from the urn and it is desired to know the probability that 3 of them have the same color as the ball which was drawn first. After the first ball has been drawn, 5 others are drawn from the 31 that remain, of which 7 are of the same color as the first. The total number of possibilities is thus given by the number of ways in which 5 balls can be chosen from a set of 31, and it is equal to

$$\frac{31 \cdot 30 \cdot 29 \cdot 28 \cdot 27}{1 \cdot 2 \cdot 3 \cdot 4 \cdot 5}$$

The number of favorable cases is obtained by multiplying the number of ways in which 3 balls can be chosen from the 7 having the same color as the first by the number of ways in which 2 balls can be chosen from the 24 having a color different from that of the first. Thus, the total number of favorable cases is given by

$$\frac{7 \cdot 6 \cdot 5}{1 \cdot 2 \cdot 3} \cdot \frac{24 \cdot 23}{1 \cdot 2}$$

and the desired probability equals the quotient obtained by dividing the number of favorable cases by the total number of cases, namely,

$$\frac{7 \cdot 6 \cdot 5 \cdot 24 \cdot 23}{31 \cdot 30 \cdot 29 \cdot 28 \cdot 27} \cdot \frac{1 \cdot 2 \cdot 3 \cdot 4 \cdot 5}{1 \cdot 2 \cdot 3 \cdot 1 \cdot 2}$$

Simple cancellations yield

$$\frac{24 \cdot 23 \cdot 5}{31 \cdot 29 \cdot 27 \cdot 2} = \frac{4 \cdot 23 \cdot 5}{31 \cdot 29 \cdot 9} = \frac{460}{8,091}$$

and the desired probability falls between 1/17 and 1/18.

2.6 *Other Problems*

PROBLEM 10. *Study the problem of the pool (Problem 3) by the method of composite probabilities.* The first game is played by A and B and we designate this by AB. If A wins, B leaves the game and he is replaced by C; otherwise, A leaves the game and he is replaced by C. Thus, for the second game we have the two expressions AC' and BC', where the prime indicates that C has just entered the game. If A wins in the combination AC' the game is finished; otherwise, A leaves the game and he is replaced by B; for the third game one thus has the combinations CB' and CA'. Similarly, for the next few games one has BA' and AB', AC' and BC', CB' and CA', ..., and it can be seen that the combinations recur periodically.

For each game, starting with the second, there is one chance in two that the match will end and one chance in two that it will continue. Thus, the probability that the match will end with the second game is 1/2, the probability that it will end with the third game is 1/4, the probability that it will end with the fourth game is 1/8, and so forth.

What is the probability of each of the alternatives described above? In each game in which the match does not end the two possibilities are equally probable, and it follows that the probability is 1/4 for the second game, 1/8 for the third game, and so on. Furthermore, the probability that a specified player will win in one of these situations is 1/2 if his letter does not have a prime, and it is 0 if his letter has a prime. The probability that a player wins through one of the combinations where his letter does not have a prime is, thus, 1/4 if the combination appears in the second game, 1/8 if it appears in the third game, 1/16 if it appears in the fourth game, and so on. Consequently, the probabilities of winning are as shown in the following table.

Number of game	A	B	C
2	1/4	1/4	0
3	0	0	$1/8 + 1/8 = 1/4$
4	1/16	1/16	0
5	1/32	1/32	0
6	0	0	$1/64 + 1/64 = 1/32$
. . . .			
$3n + 1$	$1/2^{3n+1}$	$1/2^{3n+1}$	0
$3n + 2$	$1/2^{3n+2}$	$1/2^{3n+2}$	0
$3n + 3$	0	0	$1/2^{3n+3} + 1/2^{3n+3} = 1/2^{3n+2}$

The probability that A (or B) wins in at most $3n$ games is thus

$$\frac{1}{4} + \frac{1}{16} + \frac{1}{32} + \frac{1}{128} + \frac{1}{256} + \ldots + \frac{1}{2^{3n-2}} + \frac{1}{2^{3n-1}}$$

$$= \frac{1}{4} + \frac{3}{2}\left(\frac{1}{16} + \frac{1}{128} + \ldots + \frac{1}{2^{3n-2}}\right)$$

and upon summing the geometric progression

$$\frac{1}{4} + \frac{3}{2} \cdot \frac{\dfrac{1}{16} - \dfrac{1}{2^{3n+1}}}{1 - \dfrac{1}{8}} = \frac{1}{4} + \frac{3}{28} - \frac{3}{7 \cdot 2^{3n-1}} = \frac{5}{14} - \frac{3}{7 \cdot 2^{3n-1}}$$

The probability that C wins in at most $3n$ games is

$$\frac{1}{4} + \frac{1}{32} + \ldots + \frac{1}{2^{3n-1}} = \frac{\dfrac{1}{4} - \dfrac{1}{2^{3n+2}}}{1 - \dfrac{1}{8}} = \frac{2}{7} - \frac{1}{7 \cdot 2^{3n-1}}$$

If n increases indefinitely, that is, if one does not restrict the number of games, these probabilities approach the values 5/14 and 2/7, which we obtained in Section 1.7. The probability that one of the players wins in $3n$ games or less is

$$\frac{5}{14} - \frac{3}{7 \cdot 2^{3n-1}} + \frac{5}{14} - \frac{3}{7 \cdot 2^{3n-1}} + \frac{2}{7} - \frac{1}{7 \cdot 2^{3n-1}} = 1 - \frac{1}{2^{3n-1}}$$

and it equals one minus the probability that the match will last for more than $3n$ games.

The preceding analysis is longer, but more instructive, than the method of Section 1.7. For example, it lends itself to solving problems such as the following.

PROBLEM 11. *What are the mathematical expectations of players A and C, if the amount of money the winner receives equals the number of games played?* Under these conditions the mathematical expectation of A is

$$\frac{2}{4} + \frac{4}{16} + \frac{5}{32} + \frac{7}{128} + \cdots + \frac{3n-2}{2^{3n-2}} + \frac{3n-1}{2^{3n-1}} + \cdots$$

namely

$$\frac{1}{2} + \sum_{n=2}^{\infty} \frac{9n-5}{2^{3n-1}} = \frac{1}{2} + \frac{9}{4} \sum_{n=2}^{\infty} \frac{n}{8^{n-1}} - \frac{5}{4} \sum_{n=2}^{\infty} \frac{1}{8^{n-1}}$$

$$= \frac{1}{2} + \frac{9 \cdot 15}{4 \cdot 49} - \frac{5 \cdot 1}{4 \cdot 7}$$

$$= 1 + \frac{1}{98}$$

The mathematical expectation of C is

$$\frac{3}{4} + \frac{6}{32} + \cdots + \frac{3n}{2^{3n-1}} + \cdots = \frac{3}{4} \sum_{n=1}^{\infty} \frac{n}{8^{n-1}} = 1 - \frac{1}{49}$$

and this is less than that of A. However, the disadvantage is much less than it was in the case where the winnings were fixed.

The sum of the mathematical expectation of the three players A, B, and C is given by

$$1 + \frac{1}{98} + 1 + \frac{1}{98} + 1 - \frac{1}{49} = 3$$

and this result could have been obtained directly. The probability that the match ends with the nth game is $1/2^{n-1}$, in which case the gain is equal to n.

Thus, the total mathematical expectation of the three players is*

$$\sum_{n=2}^{\infty} \frac{n}{2^{n-1}} = 3$$

PROBLEM 12. *What advantage should the first two players give the third in order to make the game of the pool equitable, assuming equal stakes?* Suppose that when C plays against either A or B, the probability that he wins is given by some number p greater than $1/2$; when A and B play, each has a probability of $1/2$. It is desired to determine p in such a way that the game is equitable, that is, in such a way that the probability of ultimately winning is $1/3$ for each player.

Under these conditions, the probability that the match ends with the nth game is modified; reasoning like that used on page 22 leads to the result that the probability that C will ultimately win is

$$p^2\left[1 + \frac{p(1 - p)}{2} + \frac{p^2(1 - p)^2}{4} + \frac{p^3(1 - p)^3}{8} + \cdots\right]$$

Putting this expression equal to $1/3$, one finally obtains p by solving the equation

$$5p^2 + p - 2 = 0$$

The positive root of this equation is approximately 0.54, and we conclude that C will have to have slightly better than 54 chances in 100 when he plays with either A or B.

---

* Here and in the preceding calculation we are making use of the formula

$$\frac{1}{(1 - x)^2} = 1 + 2x + 3x^2 + 4x^3 + \cdots$$

CHAPTER THREE

Approximation Formulas

3.1 *Objectives of this Chapter*

We have already seen that in order to determine the values of different probabilities one is led to calculate the number of various kinds of combinations; these calculations involved the product of the first m positive integers. In fact, we found that

$$C_m^p = \frac{m!}{p!(m-p)!}$$

Using the factorial notation, one can also write expressions of the form $1 \cdot 3 \cdot 5 \cdot \ldots \cdot (2m-1)$, namely, products of the first m odd integers; in that case one has

$$1 \cdot 3 \cdot 5 \cdot \ldots \cdot (2m-1) = \frac{(2m)!}{2 \cdot 4 \cdot 6 \cdot \ldots \cdot 2m} = \frac{(2m)!}{2^m \cdot m!}$$

This explains why great importance is attached to the rapid evaluation of $m!$, even though the result may only be approximate. In connection with this, it is important to state precisely what we mean here by "approximate." The "approximate values" we shall give for $m!$ can actually differ considerably from the exact value in the sense that the *difference* between the approximate value and the exact value can be quite large. In fact, the difference increases with n. On the other hand, the *ratio* of the approximate value to the exact value will be close to 1, and it will approach 1 when n becomes large. In other words, although the absolute error may be large, the relative error will be very small. Note that it is the relative error which is important in problems of probability, since probabilities are usually given by quotients of products of factorials.

3.2 *Stirling's Formula*

The following formula, due to Stirling, is most often used in practice to approximate $n!$:

$$n! = n^n e^{-n} \sqrt{2\pi n}\,(1 + \epsilon_n)$$

In this formula,* n is an arbitrary whole number, e is the base of natural logarithms ($e = 2.71828\ldots$), π is the ratio of the circumference to the diameter of a circle ($\pi = 3.14159\ldots$), and ϵ_n is a number which varies with n, but which *tends to zero when n increases indefinitely.* In certain applications it is useful to know that $n \cdot \epsilon_n$ tends to $1/12$ when n becomes large; in that case one lets $12n \cdot \epsilon_n = 1 + \theta_n$.

3.3 *Application to the Equality of Players in Heads or Tails*

To give an immediate application, let us calculate the probability that two players are even after having played $2n$ games of heads or tails, namely, that there have been n heads and n tails. According to what we have already shown, this probability is given by

$$\frac{1}{2^{2n}} \cdot C_{2n}^n = \frac{(2n)!}{2^{2n}(n!)^2}$$

If we now use the formula of Section 3.2, we obtain

$$\frac{(2n)^{2n} \cdot e^{-2n} \cdot \sqrt{4\pi n} \cdot \left(1 + \dfrac{1 + \theta_{2n}}{24n}\right)}{2^{2n} \cdot n^{2n} \cdot e^{-2n} \cdot 2\pi n \cdot \left(1 + \dfrac{1 + \theta_n}{12n}\right)}$$

which can be written as

$$\frac{1 + \epsilon_n}{\sqrt{\pi n}}$$

where $1 + \epsilon_n$ tends to 1 when n approaches infinity, that is, ϵ_n approaches zero. It can be seen that this probability decreases when n increases, but that it decreases more slowly.

To measure the degree of approximation for small values of n, let us refer again to Pascal's triangle. For $n = 5$ one has

$$\frac{252}{1,024} = \frac{1 + \epsilon_5}{5\pi}$$

which gives approximately $1 + \epsilon_5 = 0.975$. Thus, the *relative error* ϵ_5 is approximately $1/40$.

---

* Derivations of this formula may be found in more advanced texts; however, one can apply it without knowing how it is proved.

If one substitutes 1.772 for $\sqrt{\pi}$, it can be seen that for $n = 100$ the probability of getting 100 heads and 100 tails is

$$\frac{1}{10 \cdot 1.772} = \frac{1}{17.72}$$

or approximately 1/18. Similarly, the probability of getting 10,000 heads in 20,000 games is approximately 1/177.

Thus, the probability that a player of heads or tails is *even* decreases when the number of games, fixed in advance, is increased; for 200 games the probability that the players are even is 1/18, for 20,000 games it is 1/177, and for 2,000,000 games it is only 1/1,772. We would be committing a serious error, like the one indicated in Section 1.9, if we arrived at the following conclusion: As it happens often enough that the game is in equilibrium, one can always suppose that the game starts again at that precise moment and, hence, that the probability (of an equilibrium) remains constant. Actually, long runs favoring one player are improbable, but they will nevertheless happen if the game lasts for a sufficient length of time; thus, there will be long periods of time during which there is no equilibrium.

Of course, this decrease in the chances for an equilibrium must be taken into account when calculating the mathematical expectation of a spectator who is to receive a certain fixed amount (equal to unity) each time the two players are even. We shall actually calculate this mathematical expectation, treating the approximation formula as exact; the error will be very small, and it would be noticeable only for very small values of n.

The mathematical expectation equals the sum of the mathematical expectations corresponding to the situations where an equilibrium can occur, namely, after 2 games, after 4 games, . . . , or after $2n$ games. For $2n$ games its total value is thus

$$\frac{1}{\sqrt{\pi}}\left(1 + \frac{1}{\sqrt{2}} + \frac{1}{\sqrt{3}} + \ldots + \frac{1}{\sqrt{n}}\right)$$

and one can obtain an approximation for the expression in parentheses by replacing it with the integral

$$\int_0^n \frac{dx}{\sqrt{x}} = 2\sqrt{n}$$

An approximation to the desired mathematical expectation is thus given by

$$\frac{2}{\sqrt{\pi}}\sqrt{n}$$

which is close to $1.128\sqrt{n}$. For 200 games the mathematical expectation is 11; for 800 games it is only twice as much, namely, 22; for two million games it is 1,128.

Suppose that Paul plays series of 1,000 games of heads or tails, where each series is looked upon separately; that is, after each series is finished one starts counting the results from zero. Paul pays $20 for the privilege of playing each series, and he receives $1 each time an equilibrium occurs. Note that this would most likely be an advantageous bargain; by virtue of the law of large numbers (see next chapter) one might say that it will definitely be advantageous, provided the number of series is sufficiently large. If he plays 2,000 series (and, hence, 2,000,000 individual games), he has to pay $40,000, but he would probably make a profit of many thousands of dollars. On the other hand, if the two million games were regarded as a *single series*, he could expect to receive only $1,128, and it would be foolish to pay even $2,000, not to mention $40,000, for the privilege of playing the game. It can be seen from this concrete example how erroneous it would be to decompose the series of 2,000,000 games into series of approximately 2,000 each under the pretext that an equilibrium will *on the average* occur more than 1,000 times in 2,000,000 games. Actually, the irregularity in returns to equilibrium are much larger. It will frequently happen that during some thousands of games there are so many instances where the players are even that Paul will think that he can quickly get rich; then one of the players has an exceptional run of luck, and a return to equilibrium becomes less and less likely, as it would require an exceptional run of luck in the opposite direction. It can thus happen that Paul will not receive a cent for tens of thousands of games. Eventually, there will probably be a return to equilibrium and, most likely, it will be followed by a period during which Paul will win. Cycles of this kind will recur again and again. If we refer to a run as exceptional if it contains, say, 50 successive heads or tails, it may well happen that there will be even more exceptional runs, exceeding 200 or 300, if one plays hundreds of thousands of games. Such runs will be followed by extremely long periods, maybe 100,000 games or more, during which there is no return to equilibrium.

3.4 *A Second Approximation*

In place of the formula of Section 3.2 one can obtain a better approximation by writing

$$(1) \qquad\qquad n! = n^n e^{-n} \sqrt{2\pi n}\; f(n)$$

where

$$(2)\quad \log f(n+1) - \log f(n)$$

$$= -\frac{1}{12n^2} + \frac{1}{12n^3} - \frac{3}{40n^4} + \cdots + \frac{(-1)^{p+1}(p-1)}{2p(p+1)n^p} + \cdots$$

and

$$(3) \qquad\qquad \lim_{n \to \infty} f(n) = 1$$

These three relations enable one to obtain approximations which are as close as desired. The formula of Section 3.2 is obtained by using the first term of (2); to include the succeeding terms, we shall use the following result previously obtained:

(4)
$$f(n) = 1 + \frac{1}{12n} + \frac{1 + \theta_n}{\alpha n^2}$$

Here θ_n tends to zero when n increases indefinitely, and α is a coefficient which will have to be calculated. Taking logarithms, we have

(5)
$$\log f(n) = \frac{1}{12n} + \frac{1 + \theta_n}{\alpha n^2} - \frac{1}{2}\left(\frac{1}{12n} + \frac{1 + \theta_n}{\alpha n^2}\right)^2 + \cdots$$
$$= \frac{1}{12n} + \left(\frac{1}{\alpha} - \frac{1}{288}\right)\frac{1}{n^2} + \cdots$$

omitting terms of order $1/n^3$ or less. One thus has

$$\log f(n + 1) - \log f(n) = \frac{1}{12}\left(\frac{1}{n + 1} - \frac{1}{n}\right)$$
$$+ \left(\frac{1}{\alpha} - \frac{1}{288}\right)\left(\frac{1}{(n + 1)^2} - \frac{1}{n^2}\right) + \cdots$$

But

$$\frac{1}{n + 1} - \frac{1}{n} = -\frac{1}{n^2} + \frac{1}{n^3} - \frac{1}{n^4} + \cdots$$

$$\frac{1}{(n + 1)^2} - \frac{1}{n^2} = -\frac{2}{n^3} + \frac{3}{n^4} - \frac{4}{n^5} + \cdots$$

and, using only the terms in $1/n^2$ and $1/n^3$, we obtain

$$\log f(n + 1) - \log f(n) = -\frac{2}{12n^2} + \left(\frac{1}{12} - \frac{2}{\alpha} + \frac{2}{144}\right)\frac{1}{n^3} + \cdots$$

Comparing this result with (2), we find that the value of α is 288. We shall not rewrite formula (4), since all the important formulas obtained in this chapter will be summarized below.

3.5 *Summary of Formulas*

In some cases it is sufficient to use the formula

(1)
$$n! = n^n e^{-n}\sqrt{2\pi n}\,(1 + \epsilon_n)$$

where it is known that ϵ_n tends to zero when n is increased indefinitely. This formula can also be written in the form

(2)
$$\log n! = \left(n + \frac{1}{2}\right) \cdot \log n - n + \log\sqrt{2\pi} + \epsilon_n'$$

where ϵ'_n tends to zero when n becomes infinite. A first approximation of ϵ_n is obtained by putting

$$\epsilon_n = \frac{1 + \theta_n}{12n}$$

which yields

(3)
$$n! = n^n e^{-n} \sqrt{2\pi n} \left(1 + \frac{1 + \theta_n}{12n}\right)$$

and

(4)
$$\log n! = \left(n + \frac{1}{2}\right) \cdot \log n - n + \log \sqrt{2\pi} + \frac{1 + \theta'_n}{12n}$$

Finally, a second approximation gives

(5)
$$n! = n^n e^{-n} \sqrt{2\pi} \left(1 + \frac{1}{12n} + \frac{1 + \eta_n}{288n^2}\right)$$

It is remarkable that formula (4) gives as good an approximation as formula (5), if one assumes that $n\theta'_n$ tends to zero when n is increased indefinitely; this follows from formula (5) of the preceding section, where the assumption that $n\theta'_n$ tends to zero led to $\alpha = 288$; the term in $1/n^2$ disappears. Omitting the necessary calculations, let us also give the following third approximation for $\log n!$:

(6)
$$\log n! = \left(n + \frac{1}{2}\right) \cdot \log n - n + \log \sqrt{2\pi} + \frac{1}{12n} - \frac{1 + \theta_n}{360n^3}$$

Let us also mention the following formula, due to Forsyth:

(7)
$$n! = \sqrt{2\pi} \left[\frac{\sqrt{n^2 + n + \frac{1}{6}}}{e}\right]^{n + \frac{1}{2}}$$

which follows from (6) if one substitutes $1/144$ for $(1 + \theta_n)/360$. Using formula (7), the error in $\log n!$ is thus about $\dfrac{1}{240n^3}$; using formula (4), the error is about $\dfrac{1}{360n^3}$.

Practically speaking, formulas (1) and (2) are quite adequate for most applications; formulas (3), (4), (5), and (6) are used mainly in theoretical research.

CHAPTER FOUR

Further Study of the Game of Heads or Tails

4.1 A Fundamental Formula

Let us investigate the probability of getting $m - h$ heads and $m + h$ tails in $2m$ games of heads or tails, namely, the probability

$$p = \frac{1}{2^{2m}} \cdot \frac{(2m)!}{(m - h)!(m + h)!}$$

First we shall calculate $\log p$, evaluating the factorials by means of formula (4). Designating by θ a number between 0 and 1 (which need not be the same in the various formulas), we have

$$\log p = -2m \cdot \log 2 + \left(2m + \frac{1}{2}\right) \cdot \log 2m - 2m + \log \sqrt{2\pi} + \frac{1 + \theta}{24m}$$

$$- \left(m - h + \frac{1}{2}\right) \cdot \log (m - h) + (m - h) - \log \sqrt{2\pi} - \frac{1 + \theta'}{12(m - h)}$$

$$- \left(m + h + \frac{1}{2}\right) \cdot \log (m + h) + (m + h) - \log \sqrt{2\pi} - \frac{1 + \theta''}{12(m + h)}$$

To simplify this formula, note that $\log 2m = \log 2 + \log m$ and that the coefficient $2m + \frac{1}{2}$ of $\log m$ can be written as

$$2m + \frac{1}{2} = -\frac{1}{2} + \left(m - h + \frac{1}{2}\right) + \left(m + h + \frac{1}{2}\right)$$

Thus

$$\log p = -\frac{1}{2}\log m - \log \sqrt{\pi} + \epsilon_m + \left(m - h + \frac{1}{2}\right)[\log m - \log (m - h)]$$

$$+ \left(m + h + \frac{1}{2}\right)[\log m - \log (m + h)]$$

where

$$\epsilon_m = \frac{1 + \theta}{24m} - \frac{1 + \theta''}{12(m + h)} - \frac{1 + \theta'}{12(m - h)}$$

This last quantity is very small when m and $m - h$ are large.

Making use of the series

$$\log m - \log (m - h) = -\log \left(1 - \frac{h}{m}\right) = \frac{h}{m} + \frac{h^2}{2m^2} + \frac{h^3}{3m^3} + \cdots$$

$$\log m - \log (m + h) = -\log \left(1 + \frac{h}{m}\right) = -\frac{h}{m} + \frac{h^2}{2m^2} - \frac{h^3}{3m^3} + \cdots$$

which converge for $h < m$, we obtain

$$\left(m - h + \frac{1}{2}\right)[\log m - \log (m - h)] = h + \frac{h^2}{2m} + \frac{h^3}{3m^2} + \cdots$$

$$- \frac{h^2}{m} - \frac{h^3}{2m^2} - \cdots + \frac{1}{2}\cdot\frac{h}{m} + \frac{1}{2}\cdot\frac{h^2}{2m^2} + \cdots$$

The product $(m + h + \frac{1}{2})[\log m - \log (m + h)]$ is obtained by substituting $-h$ for h in this last result, and we finally have

$$\log p = -\frac{1}{2}\cdot\log m - \log \sqrt{\pi} + \epsilon_m - \frac{h^2}{m} + \frac{h^3}{2m^2} + \cdots$$

The terms that are omitted contain m with an exponent of at least 3 in the denominator, and the exponent of h in the numerator exceeds the exponent of m at most by 1.

Since h is always less than m, these terms are numerically less than the negative term $-h^2/m$; furthermore, when h^2 is large compared to m, this negative term is numerically large, and hence $\log p$ is very small. Assuming that $h^3 > m^2$, we have

$$\frac{h^2}{m} > \frac{h^2}{h\sqrt{h}} = \sqrt{h}$$

and $p < e^{-\sqrt{h}} < e^{-\sqrt{m}}$. For instance, if $m = 1,000$ and $h > 100$, p is less than e^{-10}; if $m = 1,000,000$ and $h > 10,000$, p is less than e^{-100}. The value of p is so small in each of these examples that there is no need to evaluate it precisely.

Let us continue our calculations with the approximate formula, assuming now that $h^3 < m^2$; omitting all terms containing m^k with $k \geqslant 2$ in the denominator, it follows that

$$\log p = -\frac{1}{2} \cdot \log m\pi + \epsilon_m - \frac{h^2}{m}$$

and, hence, that

$$p = \frac{1}{\sqrt{m\pi}} e^{-h^2/m}(1 + \eta_m)$$

where ϵ_m and η_m are numbers which tend to zero when n is increased indefinitely.

This formula generalizes the result obtained in Section 3.3 for $h = 0$, and it is of great importance. Let us stress the fact that it follows analytically from the formula for combinations, and that it does not entail any other assumptions.

4.2 The Unit Deviation

It is customary to modify the above formula for p by making the substitution $h = \lambda\sqrt{m}$, where h is called the *deviation* (from m). The quantity $\sqrt{m}$ is called the *unit deviation** and λ is called the *relative deviation*. If we make this substitution, we obtain

$$p = \frac{1}{\sqrt{m\pi}} e^{-\lambda^2}(1 + \eta_m)$$

and it can be seen that the exponential term depends only on the relative deviation λ, which is essentially the reason for making this substitution.

When h and m are both very large, one can vary h by several units without appreciably affecting λ. Thus, let us designate by h_1 and h_2 two whole numbers that are fairly close, and let us look for the probability that the deviation h is contained between h_1 and h_2. More precisely, let us look for the probability that $h_1 \leqslant h < h_2$. If we write $h_1 = \lambda_1\sqrt{m}$ and $h_2 = \lambda_2\sqrt{m}$, assuming that λ_1 and λ_2 are so close that they can be replaced, without error, by some number λ in the exponential $e^{-\lambda^2}$, the desired probability equals the sum of as many terms as there are values of h. Since these terms are all equal, the value of the probability is

$$P = (h_2 - h_1)\frac{1}{\sqrt{m\pi}} \cdot e^{-\lambda^2}(1 + \eta_m)$$

which can also be written as

$$P = \frac{\lambda_2 - \lambda_1}{\sqrt{\pi}} \cdot e^{-\lambda^2}(1 + \eta_m)$$

---

* It should be observed that if the unit deviation is divided by $\sqrt{2}$, one obtains the *standard deviation*, which is more commonly used in today's literature on probability and statistics.

This result is remarkable, insofar as the formula involves only the relative deviation λ. It exhibits a special kind of homogeneity peculiar to problems of probability.

To illustrate, let us put $2m = 200$, $h_1 = 5$, and $h_2 = 7$. Thus, we want to find the probability of getting either 105 or 106 heads in 200 games, that is, at least 105 heads and fewer than 107. Having $\sqrt{m} = 10$, $\lambda_1 = 0.5$, and $\lambda_2 = 0.7$, it can be seen that the value of λ^2 must fall between 0.25 and 0.36. Putting it equal to 0.30, we get

$$\frac{e^{-\lambda^2}}{\sqrt{\pi}} = \frac{e^{-0.3}}{\sqrt{\pi}} = 0.42$$

and the desired probability is approximately

$$P = (\lambda_2 - \lambda_1)(0.42) = (0.2)(0.42) = 0.084$$

Had we used $2m = 20{,}000$, $h_1 = 50$, and $h_2 = 70$, the values of λ_1 and λ_2, and hence also the probability, would have been the same. Now the probability pertains to the event of getting $10{,}050, 10{,}051, \ldots,$ or $10{,}069$ heads in 20,000 games, namely, the probability of getting at least 10,050 heads and fewer than 10,070.

This example demonstrated the conditions of homogeneity: it would not be correct to say that the probability of getting 10,050 heads in 20,000 games equals that of getting 105 heads in 200 games; actually, the latter is ten times as large. Corresponding to the probability of getting 105 heads in 200 games we have, in fact, the probability of getting anywhere from 10,050 to 10,059 (or from 10,045 to 10.054 if one prefers), namely, the sum of 10 probabilities which are almost all alike.

The procedure which we have illustrated provides only a crude approximation, but it is often sufficient. To facilitate its use, we give the following table containing the values of $\dfrac{1}{\sqrt{\pi}} \cdot e^{-\lambda^2}$ for selected values of λ:

λ	$\dfrac{1}{\sqrt{\pi}} \cdot e^{-\lambda^2}$	λ	$\dfrac{1}{\sqrt{\pi}} \cdot e^{-\lambda^2}$
0.01	0.564	0.3	0.516
0.02	0.564	0.4	0.481
0.03	0.564	0.5	0.439
0.04	0.563	0.6	0.394
0.05	0.563	0.7	0.341
0.06	0.562	0.8	0.297
0.07	0.561	0.9	0.251
0.08	0.561	1.0	0.208
0.09	0.560	1.5	0.059
0.10	0.559	2.0	0.010
0.20	0.542	2.5	0.001

4.3 *Use of a Continuous Variable*

We have seen that the probability that the *relative deviation* λ is contained between λ_1 and λ_2 can be approximated by the formula

$$(1) \qquad\qquad P = (\lambda_2 - \lambda_1) \frac{1}{\sqrt{\pi}} \cdot e^{-\lambda^2}$$

where the relative deviations λ_1 and λ_2 are given by the formulas $h_2 = \lambda_2\sqrt{m}$ and $h_1 = \lambda_1\sqrt{m}$. Since h_2 and h_1 must be whole numbers, it follows that λ_1 and λ_2 cannot take on all values on a continuous scale.

However, when $\sqrt{m}$ is large, the values of λ, which vary in steps of size $1/\sqrt{m}$, may be looked upon as a continuous series, and one is led to replace formula (1) by the following formula for P:

$$(2) \qquad\qquad P = \frac{1}{\sqrt{\pi}} \int_{\lambda_1}^{\lambda_2} e^{-\lambda^2} \, d\lambda$$

It should be noted that by virtue of the Law of the Mean the value of this integral is actually given by formula (1), where λ is a certain number between λ_1 and λ_2. The advantage of formula (2) is that it does not require the assumption that λ_1 and λ_2 are close together, for if one assumes that $\lambda_1 < \lambda_2 < \lambda_3$ and puts

$$P_{1,2} = \frac{1}{\sqrt{\pi}} \int_{\lambda_1}^{\lambda_2} e^{-\lambda^2} \, d\lambda \qquad \text{and} \qquad P_{2,3} = \frac{1}{\sqrt{\pi}} \int_{\lambda_2}^{\lambda_3} e^{-\lambda^2} \, d\lambda$$

one has

$$P_{1,2} + P_{2,3} = \frac{1}{\sqrt{\pi}} \int_{\lambda_1}^{\lambda_3} e^{-\lambda^2} \, d\lambda$$

This can be generalized to any number of successive intervals of the variable λ.

The probability P that λ is contained between $-a$ and a is given by

$$P_a = \frac{1}{\sqrt{\pi}} \int_{-a}^{a} e^{-\lambda^2} \, d\lambda$$

and when a increases indefinitely, the probability tends to the limit

$$P_\infty = \frac{1}{\sqrt{\pi}} \int_{-\infty}^{\infty} e^{-\lambda^2} \, d\lambda$$

It can easily be verified that the value of this integral is 1. If we put

$$J = \frac{1}{\sqrt{\pi}} \int_{-\infty}^{\infty} e^{-x^2}\, dx = \frac{1}{\sqrt{\pi}} \int_{-\infty}^{\infty} e^{-y^2}\, dy$$

we have

$$J^2 = \frac{1}{\pi} \int_{-\infty}^{\infty} \int_{-\infty}^{\infty} e^{-x^2-y^2}\, dx\, dy$$

and, after changing to polar coordinates and integrating over the entire plane, we get

$$J^2 = \frac{1}{\pi} \int_{0}^{\infty} e^{-r^2} r\, dr \cdot \int_{0}^{2\pi} d\theta = 1$$

It is clear that if we use the exact formulas instead of the approximate formulas, the total probability that the relative deviation assumes one of the values within its domain must be equal to 1. But if we put

$$\lambda = \frac{h}{\sqrt{m}}$$

then h can vary from $-m$ to m, since $m + h$ (the number of games won) can vary from 0 to $2m$. It follows that λ can vary from $-\sqrt{m}$ to $+\sqrt{m}$ and, hence, λ^2 from 0 to m. Now, when m is sufficiently large, $e^{-\lambda^2}$ becomes negligible when λ^2 exceeds m; for example, if $m = 100$, e^{-m} is less than 10^{-43}. Such a quantity is negligible in most practical calculations; and consequently, one does not commit an error in extending the integral from $-\infty$ to ∞ instead of limiting it to the interval from $-m$ to $+m$. It is remarkable that the value of the total probability thus obtained equals 1 even though the formulas used are only approximate. This shows that the small errors committed by using the approximation of Section 4.1 are mutually compensating. As we shall see, this is very important insofar as the application of the formulas is concerned.

4.4 Definition of the Function $\theta(\lambda)$

It is customary to designate by $\theta(\lambda)$ the probability that the relative deviation is contained between $-\lambda$ and $+\lambda$; hence, one writes

$$\theta(\lambda) = \frac{1}{\sqrt{\pi}} \int_{-\lambda}^{+\lambda} e^{-\lambda^2}\, d\lambda$$

or, equivalently,

$$\theta(\lambda) = \frac{2}{\sqrt{\pi}} \int_{0}^{\lambda} e^{-\lambda^2}\, d\lambda$$

Special tables of the function $\theta(\lambda)$ have been calculated, and they are widely used in applications of the calculus of probability. Some values of this function are given in the table which follows; it also contains the values of the difference $1 - \theta(\lambda)$, namely,

$$1 - \theta(\lambda) = \frac{2}{\sqrt{\pi}} \int_{\lambda}^{\infty} e^{-\lambda^2} \, d\lambda$$

λ	$\theta(\lambda)$	$1 - \theta(\lambda)$
0.1	0.1125	0.8875
0.2	0.2227	0.7773
0.3	0.3286	0.6714
0.4	0.4284	0.5716
0.4769	0.5000	0.5000
0.5	0.5205	0.4795
0.6	0.6039	0.3961
0.7	0.6778	0.3222
0.8	0.7421	0.2597
0.9	0.7969	0.2031
1.0	0.8427	0.1573
1.1	0.8802	0.1198
1.163	0.9000	0.1000
1.5	0.9661	0.0339
1.821	0.9900	0.0100
2.0	0.9953	0.0047
2.327	0.9990	0.0010
2.751	0.9999	0.0001
3.0	0.999979	0.000021
3.123	0.99999	0.00001
3.46	0.999999	0.000001
3.763	0.9999999	0.0000001
4.0	0.999999985	0.000000015

This table shows how rapidly $\theta(\lambda)$ approaches 1; for $\lambda = 4$ we have $1 - \theta(\lambda) = 1.5/10^8$, and this quantity is negligible in most practical applications. A more complete table may be found in Appendix IV.

By the use of these tables, various questions arising in connection with the game of heads or tails can be resolved to a sufficient degree of approximation. The following are some examples.

4.5 Applications Based On $\theta(\lambda)$

PROBLEM 16. *What is the probability of getting more than 110 heads in 200 games of heads or tails?*

Substituting $h = 10$ and $m = 100$ gives $\lambda = h/\sqrt{m} = 1$ and, according to the table the probability that the relative deviation exceeds 1 is $1 - \theta(1) = 0.157$.* One must be careful here to distinguish between the case where one

---

* It would have been more rigorous to put $h = 10.5$, in order to give λ the mean of the values corresponding to $h = 10$ and $h = 11$. We shall neglect this correction, but it should be used by the reader who wants to perform the calculations with greater precision.

has more than 110 heads and the case where one has either more than 110 heads or more than 110 tails. To obtain the required probability, the preceding probability must be divided by 2, and we obtain 0.078, or approximately 1/13.

PROBLEM 17. *What is the probability that in 20,000 games of heads or tails the absolute deviation exceeds 300, namely, that there are anywhere from 9,700 to 10,300 heads?*

The relative deviation is $300/\sqrt{10,000}$, and the probability that this value is exceeded is $1 - \theta(3) = 0.000021$. Thus, there is approximately 1 chance in 50,000 that the given event will occur.

4.6 *The Most Probable, Probable, and Median Deviations*

The probability that the deviation is contained between λ_1 and λ_2 is given by

$$\frac{1}{2}\left[\theta(\lambda_2) - \theta(\lambda_1)\right] = \frac{1}{\sqrt{\pi}} \int_{\lambda_1}^{\lambda_2} e^{-\lambda^2}\, d\lambda$$

If the interval $\lambda_2 - \lambda_1$ is constant, this probability decreases when the value of λ is increased. It is greatest for $\lambda = 0$ and, in other words, *the zero deviation is the most probable deviation.* It is important to amplify the meaning of this last statement. Suppose that one plays a great many series of 200 games of heads or tails and that one records in each case the total number of heads. If there are 100 heads the deviation is 0, if there are 101 heads the deviation is $+1$, if there are 99 heads the deviation is -1, etc. In a large number of series, the 0 deviation will occur most often; more frequently than a deviation of $+1$ or a deviation of -1, *but not more frequently than these two deviations combined.* Besides, the formulas for combinations give the ratio of the probability of a zero deviation to that of a deviation of $+1$ more precisely than the approximate formulas; it equals

$$C_{200}^{100}/C_{200}^{101} = 101/100 = 1.01$$

The name *probable deviation* or *mean value of the deviation* is given to the sum of the products obtained by multiplying each possible deviation by its probability. In other words, *the probable deviation is the mathematical expectation of a player who always receives an amount equal to the deviation.* It is important to state precisely whether one takes the algebraic value of each deviation or its absolute value. In the first case, the desired quantity would evidently equal zero, since the negative deviations are as probable as the positive deviations. Thus, one usually refers to the second case, that is, one takes the *absolute values of the deviations.* The value of the probable deviation is thus given by the integral

$$\frac{2}{\sqrt{\pi}} \int_0^{\infty} \lambda \cdot e^{-\lambda^2}\, d\lambda = \frac{1}{\sqrt{\pi}}$$

and, in other words, the mean value of the relative deviation is $1/\sqrt{\pi} = 0.5663$. The corresponding value of the absolute deviation is obtained by multiplying this value by the unit deviation $\sqrt{m}$. Thus, for a series of 20,000 games, the mean value of the deviation is $100/\sqrt{\pi} = 56.63$.

This is the mathematical expectation of a person who always receives an amount equal to the absolute deviation; it is not the deviation which occurs with the greatest frequency—that is the zero deviation.

The name *median deviation* will be given to the value which is such that there is a fifty-fifty chance that it will be exceeded. Thus, the median deviation corresponds to the value of λ for which $\theta(\lambda) = 1/2$, and it can be seen from the table of Section 4.4 that this value is $\lambda = 0.4769$. The value of the median deviation itself is obtained by multiplying this quantity by $\sqrt{m}$, and for the preceding example ($2m = 20,000$) we obtain 47.69.

Thus, for 20,000 games of heads or tails it is an even-money bet that the deviation will exceed 47 (or that it will be 47 or less). It can also be seen that the median deviation is always less than the probable deviation; their ratio is approximately 0.845.

4.7 *The Mean Value of a Function*

In general, the mean (or probable) value of a function $f(\lambda)$ of the deviation λ is defined as the sum of the products obtained by multiplying all possible values of the function by their respective probabilities. Designating this value by $\mathbf{m}[f(\lambda)]$ we have

$$\mathbf{m}[f(\lambda)] = \frac{1}{\sqrt{\pi}} \int_{-\infty}^{\infty} f(\lambda)e^{-\lambda^2}\, d\lambda$$

and, in particular,

$$\mathbf{m}(1) = \frac{1}{\sqrt{\pi}} \int_{-\infty}^{\infty} e^{-\lambda^2}\, d\lambda = 1$$

$$\mathbf{m}(\lambda) = \frac{1}{\sqrt{\pi}} \int_{-\infty}^{\infty} \lambda \cdot e^{-\lambda^2}\, d\lambda = 0$$

$$\mathbf{m}(|\lambda|) = \frac{1}{\sqrt{\pi}} \int_{-\infty}^{\infty} |\lambda| \cdot e^{-\lambda^2}\, d\lambda = \frac{1}{\sqrt{\pi}}$$

The first of these results expresses the obvious fact that if a quantity is constant, its mean value is equal to that same constant. The two other equations express the results obtained in the preceding section.

Let us now calculate the mean value of λ^2, that is, the mean value of the square of the deviation. Making the necessary substitution we obtain

$$\mathbf{m}(\lambda^2) = \frac{1}{\sqrt{\pi}} \int_{-\infty}^{\infty} \lambda^2 \cdot e^{-\lambda^2}\, d\lambda$$

and it can be shown that $\mathbf{m}(\lambda^2) = 1/2$, if we make use of the fact that

$$J_2 = \int_0^\infty \lambda^2 \cdot e^{-\lambda^2}\, d\lambda = \frac{1}{4}\sqrt{\pi} \qquad *$$

If one considers the absolute deviations $h = \lambda\sqrt{m}$ instead of the relative deviations, one obtains $\mathbf{m}(h^2) = m/2$. It is interesting to compare the mean of the squares of the deviations with the square of the mean of their absolute values. Actually calculating the ratio of these two quantities, we get

$$\frac{[\mathbf{m}(|h|)]^2}{\mathbf{m}(h^2)} = \frac{(\sqrt{m}/\sqrt{\pi})^2}{m/2} = \frac{2}{\pi}$$

This remarkable result, which contains no reference to the deviations, may be verified experimentally.

We shall return to this question in the next chapter, in connection with problems that are more general than those by the posed game of heads or tails.

---

* In general, if

$$J_n = \int_0^\infty \lambda^n \cdot e^{-\lambda^2}\, d\lambda$$

these integrals can be evaluated by means of the formula

$$\frac{d}{d\lambda}\,[\lambda^{n-1}e^{-\lambda^2}] = (n-1)\lambda^{n-2}e^{-\lambda^2} - 2\lambda^n e^{-\lambda^2}$$

Integrating from 0 to ∞ gives

$$(n-1)J_{n-2} - 2J_n = 0$$

provided $n - 1 > 0$. Using this result together with the fact that $J_0 = \frac{1}{2}\sqrt{\pi}$ and $J_1 = \frac{1}{2}$, as may be verified by direct integration, we can calculate J_n for any value of n. For example,

$$J_2 = \frac{1}{4}\sqrt{\pi}, \qquad J_4 = \frac{3}{8}\sqrt{\pi}, \qquad J_6 = \frac{3\cdot 5}{16}\sqrt{\pi}, \qquad J_8 = \frac{1\cdot 3\cdot 5\cdot 7}{32}\sqrt{\pi}$$

CHAPTER FIVE

The Law of Large Numbers

5.1 *Repeated Trials—The General Case*

Let us extend the results of the preceding chapter to the case where one considers a series of trials for which the probabilities of the two alternatives are constant from trial to trial, but not necessarily equal to 1/2. We shall let p designate the probability of one of the alternatives, which we shall refer to as a *success;* $q = 1 - p$ is the probability of the other alternative, which we shall refer to as a *failure*. If there are n trials, the probability of obtaining k successes and $n - k$ failures *in a specified order* is given by $p^k(1 - p)^{n-k}$; if the order is not specified, one must multiply this number by the total number of combinations C_n^k, and one thus obtains the value

$$P = \frac{n!}{k!(n - k)!} p^k(1 - p)^{n-k}$$

For example, the probability of getting exactly twice the number 6 in three rolls of a die is

$$\frac{3!}{1!2!}\left(\frac{1}{6}\right)^2\left(\frac{5}{6}\right) = \frac{5}{72}$$

In fact, there are three possible combinations depending on whether the first, second, or third roll does not yield a 6, and the probability for each of these combinations is $(\frac{1}{6})^2(\frac{5}{6})$.

Let us now take the general expression obtained for P and try to approximate it for the case where n and k are very large. It can easily be seen that P is largest when k and $n - k$ equal np and nq, respectively, assuming that

np and nq are whole numbers. If they are not whole numbers, P is largest when k and $n - k$ equal the integers that are closest to np and nq, respectively. If we put

$$k = np + t\sqrt{n}$$

we have

$$n - k = nq - t\sqrt{n}$$

since $p + q = 1$, and hence we can write

$$\log P = \log n! - \log (np + t\sqrt{n})! - \log (nq - t\sqrt{n})!$$
$$+ k \cdot \log p + (n - k) \cdot \log q$$

Making use of formula (4) of Section 3.5, namely,

$$\log n! = \left(n + \frac{1}{2}\right) \cdot \log n - n + \log \sqrt{2\pi} + \frac{1 + \theta_n}{12n}$$

and the fact that

$$(n + 1) \cdot \log n + k \cdot \log p + (n - k) \cdot \log q$$
$$= \left(k + \frac{1}{2}\right) \cdot \log np + \left(n - k + \frac{1}{2}\right) \cdot \log nq - \frac{1}{2} \cdot \log pq$$

we obtain

$$\log P = -\frac{1}{2} \cdot \log npq - \log \sqrt{2\pi} - \left(np + t\sqrt{n} + \frac{1}{2}\right) \cdot \log \left(1 + \frac{t}{p\sqrt{n}}\right)$$
$$- \left(nq - t\sqrt{n} + \frac{1}{2}\right) \cdot \log \left(1 - \frac{t}{q\sqrt{n}}\right) + \frac{1 + \theta_n}{12n} - \frac{1 + \theta_k}{12k} - \frac{1 + \theta_{n-k}}{12(n - k)}$$

Assuming that $t/p\sqrt{n}$ and $t/q\sqrt{n}$ are less than 1, we have

$$\left(np + t\sqrt{n} + \frac{1}{2}\right) \cdot \log \left(1 + \frac{t}{p\sqrt{n}}\right)$$
$$= \left(np + t\sqrt{n} + \frac{1}{2}\right)\left(\frac{t}{p\sqrt{n}} - \frac{t^2}{2p^2n} + \frac{t^3}{3p^3n\sqrt{n}} - \cdots\right)$$

$$\left(nq - t\sqrt{n} + \frac{1}{2}\right) \cdot \log \left(1 - \frac{t}{q\sqrt{n}}\right)$$
$$= \left(nq - t\sqrt{n} + \frac{1}{2}\right)\left(-\frac{t}{q\sqrt{n}} - \frac{t^2}{2q^2n} - \frac{t^3}{3q^3n\sqrt{n}} - \cdots\right)$$

and it follows that

$$\log P = -\frac{1}{2} \cdot \log 2\pi npq - \frac{t^2}{2pq} + \frac{t^3}{6\sqrt{n}}\left(\frac{1}{p^2} - \frac{1}{q^2}\right) - \frac{t}{2\sqrt{n}}\left(\frac{1}{p} - \frac{1}{q}\right) + \cdots$$

where the terms that are omitted are much less than those that are given.

The most important among the terms that are left is

$$\frac{t^3}{6\sqrt{n}}\left(\frac{1}{p^2} - \frac{1}{q^2}\right)$$

which vanishes when $p = q$. It can easily be seen, however, that this term is negligible unless $t/p\sqrt{n}$ is not small.*

Preserving only the principal terms, we have

$$\log P = -\frac{1}{2} \cdot \log 2\pi npq - \frac{t^2}{2pq}$$

and to write this result in the notation of the preceding chapter we let $t = \lambda\sqrt{2pq}$. Here λ is the relative deviation and $t\sqrt{n} = \lambda\sqrt{2npq}$ is the absolute deviation, since the *unit deviation* is $\sqrt{2npq}$. The probability P that the relative deviation assumes the value λ may thus be written

$$P = \frac{1}{\sqrt{2\pi npq}} e^{-\lambda^2}$$

and the probability that the relative deviation is contained between λ_1 and λ_2 (supposedly close together) is given by

$$\frac{(\lambda_2 - \lambda_1)\sqrt{2npq}}{\sqrt{2\pi npq}} e^{-\lambda^2} = \frac{\lambda_2 - \lambda_1}{\sqrt{\pi}} e^{-\lambda^2}$$

This formula is exactly the same as in the special case which we examined first; only the definition of the unit deviation had to be extended. The consequences are thus the same and we shall not state them again. However, we shall devote some time to certain new consequences, known as the *law of large numbers*, or as *Bernoulli's theorem*.

5.2 The Law of Large Numbers

Let us consider n successive trials, where p and q are again the constant probabilities for a success or a failure. If the relative deviation is λ, then the number of successes is $np + \lambda\sqrt{2npq}$ and the number of failures is $nq - \lambda\sqrt{2npq}$, and their ratio is

$$\frac{np + \lambda\sqrt{2npq}}{nq - \lambda\sqrt{2npq}}$$

---

* The introduction of additional terms has the effect that the symmetrical curve of the deviations is replaced by an asymmetrical curve. Such asymmetrical curves have been studied by various mathematicians, notably by K. Pearson, but we shall not discuss them here.

Thus, the difference between this ratio and the ratio p/q of the probabilities is

$$\frac{np + \lambda\sqrt{2npq}}{nq - \lambda\sqrt{2npq}} - \frac{p}{q} = \frac{\lambda\sqrt{2npq}(p + q)}{q(nq - \lambda\sqrt{2npq})}$$

and, making use of the fact that $p + q = 1$ and cancelling the factor $\sqrt{n}$, this difference becomes

$$\frac{\lambda\sqrt{2pq}}{q^2\sqrt{n} - \lambda q\sqrt{2pq}}$$

The numerator contains the factor λ and the denominator contains in its principal term the factor $\sqrt{n}$. Hence, the difference increases with λ, and it decreases when n increases. *For a given value of λ, it tends to zero when n becomes infinite; thus, if the relative deviation λ is less than some fixed constant, the ratio of the number of successes to the number of failures tends to the ratio p/q of their respective probabilities, when the number of trials becomes infinite.* This is the law of large numbers; in this form, it simply expresses an analytical fact.

5.3 *The Theorem of Bernoulli*

If we observe that the probability that the absolute value of λ exceeds some number A is given by $1 - \theta(A)$, and that it rapidly tends to zero when A is increased indefinitely, we obtain the following result:

THEOREM OF JACQUES BERNOULLI. *Given any $\epsilon > 0$, the probability that the absolute value of the difference between the ratio of the number of successes to the number of failures and the theoretical ratio p/q exceeds ϵ tends to zero when the number of trials, n, is increased indefinitely.*

In order to express the fact that the difference obtained above exceeds ϵ, we write

$$\left| \frac{\lambda\sqrt{2pq}}{q^2\sqrt{n} - \lambda q\sqrt{2pq}} \right| > \epsilon$$

or

$$\lambda > \frac{\epsilon q^2\sqrt{n}}{\sqrt{2pq} \pm \epsilon q\sqrt{2pq}}$$

and the probability that the preceding relationship is satisfied is

$$1 - \theta\left(\frac{\epsilon q^2\sqrt{n}}{\sqrt{2pq} \pm \epsilon q\sqrt{2pq}} \right)$$

But p and q are fixed, and no matter how small ϵ might be, the product $\epsilon\sqrt{n}$ increases indefinitely with n; it follows that the probability tends very rapidly to zero. The following are some examples.

5.4 *Some Problems*

PROBLEM 18. *A die is rolled a great number of times, and in each case the probability of getting a 6 is equal to 1/6. After how many trials is there a probability less than $1/10^8$ that the difference between the ratio of the number of times the die comes up 6 to the number of times it does not come up 6 and 1/5 is greater than 1/1,000.*

For $1 - \theta(\lambda)$ to be less than $1/10^8$, λ must exceed 4. Thus, since $p = 1/6$ and $q = 5/6$, we have

$$\frac{4\sqrt{2 \cdot \dfrac{1}{6} \cdot \dfrac{5}{6}}}{\left(\dfrac{5}{6}\right)^2 \sqrt{n} - 4 \cdot \dfrac{5}{6}\sqrt{\dfrac{2 \cdot 5}{6^2}}} < \frac{1}{1,000}$$

Omitting the second term in the denominator, we get

$$n > \frac{10^6 \cdot 4^2 \cdot 2 \cdot 5 \cdot 6^4}{6^2 \cdot 5^4} = \frac{10^6 \cdot 2 \cdot 4^2 \cdot 6^2}{5^3}$$

and it is thus sufficient to take $n > 10,000,000$.

PROBLEM 19. *Peter plays an inequitable game with Paul; the stakes are equal, but the probability that Peter will win any one game is $1/2 - \alpha$, while that for Paul is $1/2 + \alpha$. How many games should they play, if the probability that Paul leaves the game with a loss is to be less than 1/1,000?*

We shall assume that α is sufficiently small so that we can omit terms in α^2. Since

$$\frac{p}{q} = \frac{\dfrac{1}{2} + \alpha}{\dfrac{1}{2} - \alpha} = \frac{1 + 2\alpha}{1 - 2\alpha} = 1 + 4\alpha + 8\alpha^2 + \ldots$$

we shall thus put p/q equal to $1 + 4\alpha$. For Paul to leave the game with a loss, it is necessary that the ratio of the number of games he has won to the number of games he has lost is less than 1; that is, it must differ from the theoretical ratio by more than 4α (in the specified sense). For the probability of this event to be less than 1/1000, one must have

$$1 - \theta(\lambda) < 1/500 \qquad \text{or} \qquad \theta(\lambda) > 0.998$$

and it follows that $\lambda > 2.2$.

We shall make no appreciable error if we replace p and q by 1/2 in the formula of Section 5.2 and if we omit the second term in the denominator. Thus,

$$\frac{\lambda \dfrac{1}{\sqrt{2}}}{\dfrac{1}{4}\sqrt{n}} = 4\alpha$$

and

$$n > \frac{(2.2)^2}{2\alpha^2}$$

since λ must exceed 2.2.

For example, if one lets $\alpha = 1/100$, one obtains

$$n > \frac{(220)^2}{2} = 24{,}200$$

so that the player with the advantage has 999 chances in 1,000 of leaving the game with a gain, provided he plays about 24,000 games.

PROBLEM 20. *Apply the preceding results to a player who always bets on red in the game of roulette.*

Among the 37 numbers 18 are red, 18 are black, and the 37th, zero, is neither red nor black. If red wins, the banker collects all the money bet on black and he doubles all the money bet on red; if zero wins, the banker collects half of all the money bet on either red or black.

Considering a player who always bets on red, we can say that his chances of winning are 18 in 36.5 and that his chances of losing are 18.5 in 36.5, since the number zero entails only half a loss.* We thus have

$$\frac{1}{2} + \alpha = \frac{18.5}{36.5} \qquad \text{or} \qquad \alpha = \frac{0.25}{36.5}$$

and, hence, the relation $n > (2.2)^2/2\alpha^2$ yields

$$n > 8(2.2)^2(36.5)^2 > 8(80.2)^2$$

It follows that if n exceeds 52,000, the banker has 999 chances in 1,000 of not losing. Actually, the chances that the banker will lose are much smaller, since he generally does not deal with a single player, but with several players, whose stakes are divided between red and black. Clearly, if the stakes are divided equally between red and black, the banker cannot possibly lose.

---

* One could also argue that if there is a zero, the player receives 1/4 of the total stake while the banker receives 3/4, and the probability of winning is thus 18.25/37. This sort of reasoning leads, essentially, to the same result as in the text. Actually, neither result is entirely correct, since the special convention concerning zero permits the application of the result of the preceding problem only in an approximate sense.

PROBLEM 21. *Referring to the inequitable game of Problem 19, for how many games is the loss which Paul has 1 chance in 4 of exceeding a maximum?*

Assuming that the relative deviation (in a specified sense) equals the median deviation, we satisfy the conditions of the problem, since the four hypotheses

$$-\infty < \lambda < -0.4769, \qquad -0.4769 < \lambda < 0$$
$$0 < \lambda < 0.4769, \qquad\qquad 0.4769 < \lambda < \infty$$

are equally probable; each of them has a probability of $1/4$. Corresponding to this value of λ, the number of games won by Peter and Paul are, respectively,

$$\left(\frac{1}{2} - \alpha\right)n + \lambda\sqrt{2npq} \qquad \text{and} \qquad \left(\frac{1}{2} + \alpha\right)n - \lambda\sqrt{2npq}$$

and Paul's loss is

$$2\lambda\sqrt{2npq} - 2\alpha n$$

provided that this quantity is positive. It will become negative when n is sufficiently large; that is, the longer the game is continued, the better will be Paul's chances of being ahead. The maximum of the preceding quantity can be obtained by equating to zero its derivative with respect to n. If we first let $p = q = 1/2$, the quantity reduces to *

$$\lambda\sqrt{2n} - 2\alpha n$$

and we obtain

$$\frac{\lambda}{\sqrt{2}\sqrt{n}} - 2\alpha = 0$$

Solving for n, we get

$$n = \frac{\lambda^2}{8\alpha^2} = \frac{(0.48)^2}{8\alpha^2}$$

in which case Paul's loss is

$$P = \lambda\sqrt{2n} - 2\alpha n = \frac{\lambda^2}{4\alpha} = \frac{(0.48)^2}{4\alpha}$$

Supposing as in Problem 20 that $\alpha = 0.25/36.5$ and replacing 0.48 and 36.5 by 0.5 and 36, respectively, we obtain

$$n = \frac{36^2}{2} = 648$$

$$P = \frac{(0.5)^2}{4\alpha} = \frac{36}{4} = 9$$

---

* It will be left to the reader to verify that these simplifications do not introduce an appreciable error.

Thus, the most favorable number of games is 648, and the loss possible 1/4 of the time is equal to 9. Let us observe that the unit deviation is $\sqrt{2npq} = 18$, while the median deviation is approximately 9. On the other hand, the banker's probability of winning is $\frac{1}{2} + \frac{1}{4 \cdot 36}$ and, theoretically, he should win $324 + 4.5$ games. The following four alternatives are now equiprobable:

1. The banker wins more than $324 + 4.5 + 9 = 324 + 13.5$ games and his winnings exceed 27.
2. The banker wins more than $324 + 4.5$ games, but less than $324 + 4.5 + 9$, and his winnings are contained between 9 and 27.
3. The banker wins less than $324 + 4.5$ games but more than $324 + 4.5 - 9$; he can win or lose, but in either case the amount is less than 9.
4. The banker wins less than $324 + 4.5 - 9$ games, and his loss is greater than 9.

As should have been expected, the over-all results are far from being unfavorable to the banker; the game is always inequitable in his favor. Nevertheless, the preceding case is the one where he is most exposed to a relatively large loss; there is 1 chance in 4 that he will lose at least 9 times the stake. If this stake constitutes a sizable part of his total fortune, he may justifiably hesitate to accept the game, even though, as a whole, it would be advantageous. On the other hand, if he has the offer to play 10,000 consecutive games *without settling accounts until the end of the game* (*or he is allowed to borrow in case of a loss*), he can accept the conditions with the almost absolute certainty of an ultimate gain (see results of Problem 20).

5.5 *When the Probability Has Two Distinct Values*

Suppose that a series of n trials can be decomposed into two groups containing, respectively, n_1 and n_2 trials, and that the probability of a success is p_1 for each of the n_1 trials in the first group and p_2 for each of the n_2 trials in the second group. For example, one might have two urns, one with a_1 white balls and b_1 black balls and the other with a_2 white balls and b_2 black balls, and draw n_1 balls from the first urn and n_2 balls from the second urn. (Each ball is replaced before the next one is drawn, in order to preserve the composition of the urns.) Considering the drawing of a white ball as a success, one thus has

$$p_1 = \frac{a_1}{a_1 + b_1} \quad \text{and} \quad p_2 = \frac{a_2}{a_2 + b_2}$$

If the drawings conformed exactly with the probabilities, the number of successes would be $n_1 p_1 + n_2 p_2$. Otherwise, it will be $n_1 p_1 + h_1$ for the first group, $n_2 p_2 + h_2$ for the second group, and hence

$$n_1 p_1 + n_2 p_2 + h_1 + h_2 = n_1 p_1 + n_2 p_2 + h$$

altogether. Letting

$$h_1 = \lambda_1 \sqrt{2n_1 p_1 q_1} \quad \text{and} \quad h_2 = \lambda_2 \sqrt{2n_2 p_2 q_2}$$

we shall now look for the probability that the deviation h has a specified value, or rather that it is contained between h and $h + dh$. This can be realized with an arbitrary value x of the deviation h_1, in which case one must have

$$h < h_1 + h_2 = x + h_2 < h + dh$$

or

$$h - x < h_2 < h - x + dh$$

If we let $h - x = \lambda \sqrt{2n_2 p_2 q_2}$, the probability that the deviation h_2 is contained between the above limits is given by

$$\frac{1}{\sqrt{\pi}} e^{-\lambda^2} d\lambda = \frac{1}{\sqrt{2\pi n_2 p_2 q_2}} e^{-\frac{(h-x)^2}{2n_2 p_2 q_2}} dh$$

This is the value of the probability corresponding to the value x of the deviation h_1. In order to get the total probability one must take the sum of the products obtained by multiplying these partial probabilities by the corresponding probabilities for x. Since the probability that x is contained between x and $x + dx$ is given by

$$\frac{1}{\sqrt{2\pi n_1 p_1 q_1}} e^{-\frac{x^2}{2n_1 p_1 q_1}} dx$$

it follows that the probability that h is contained between h and $h + dh$ is

$$\frac{dh}{\sqrt{2\pi n_1 p_1 q_1} \sqrt{2\pi n_2 p_2 q_2}} \int_{-\infty}^{\infty} e^{-\frac{x^2}{2n_1 p_1 q_1} - \frac{(h-x)^2}{2n_2 p_2 q_2}} dx$$

To simplify this expression, let us first evaluate the following integral:

$$\int_{-\infty}^{\infty} e^{-(ax^2 + bx + c)} dx$$

Making use of the identity

$$ax^2 + bx + c = a\left(x + \frac{b}{2a}\right)^2 + \frac{4ac - b^2}{4a}$$

and letting

$$y = \sqrt{a}\left(x + \frac{b}{2a}\right) \quad \text{and} \quad w = \frac{4ac - b^2}{4a}$$

we find that the integral becomes

$$\int_{-\infty}^{\infty} e^{-(ax^2 + bx + c)} dx = \frac{1}{\sqrt{a}} \int_{-\infty}^{\infty} e^{-y^2 - w} dy = \frac{e^{-w}}{\sqrt{a}} \int_{-\infty}^{\infty} e^{-y^2} dy$$

$$= \frac{\sqrt{\pi}}{\sqrt{a}} e^{-w}$$

To apply this formula let us substitute $2n_1p_1q_1 = u_1^2$ and $2n_2p_2q_2 = u_2^2$, observing that u_1 and u_2 are the unit deviations of the individual groups of trials. We now have

$$\frac{x^2}{u_1^2} + \frac{(h-x)^2}{u_2^2} = ax^2 + bx + c$$

namely

$$a = \frac{1}{u_1^2} + \frac{1}{u_2^2}, \qquad b = \frac{-2h}{u_2^2}, \qquad c = \frac{h^2}{u_2^2}$$

$$w = \frac{4ac - b^2}{4a} = \frac{h^2}{u_1^2 + u_2^2}$$

and the value of the probability becomes

$$\frac{dh}{\pi u_1 u_2} \cdot \frac{\sqrt{\pi}}{\sqrt{a}} e^{-w} = \frac{\sqrt{\pi} \cdot dh}{\pi u_1 u_2 \sqrt{\frac{1}{u_1^2} + \frac{1}{u_2^2}}} e^{-\frac{h^2}{u_1^2 + u_2^2}}$$

Finally, if we let $u^2 = u_1^2 + u_2^2$ and $h = \lambda u$, we obtain

$$\frac{1}{\sqrt{\pi}} e^{-\lambda^2} d\lambda$$

The law for the relative deviation λ is thus the same as in the case of a single group of trials, where the unit deviation u is now given by

$$u = \sqrt{u_1^2 + u_2^2} = \sqrt{2n_1p_1q_1 + 2n_2p_2q_2}$$

5.6 Substitution of One Group for Two Groups of Trials

Suppose that the numbers p and q are defined by the relations $np = n_1p_1 + n_2p_2$ and $nq = n_1q_1 + n_2q_2$, where n, n_1, n_2, p_1, q_1, p_2, and q_2 have the same significance as in the preceding section. Note that since $p_1 + q_1 = 1$, $p_2 + q_2 = 1$, and $n = n_1 + n_2$, it follows that $p + q = 1$.

If one performs n trials in which the probability for a success is p, the theoretical values of the number of successes and the number of failures are, respectively, np and nq; they are the same as in the case of the two groups of trials considered above. *However, the unit deviation will not be the same.* Designating this unit deviation by U, we have

$$U^2 = 2npq$$

On the other hand, for the case of two groups of trials we found that the unit deviation u is given by

$$u^2 = u_1^2 + u_2^2 = 2(n_1p_1q_1 + n_2p_2q_2)$$

so that

$$U^2 - u^2 = 2(npq - n_1 p_1 q_1 - n_2 p_2 q_2)$$

Multiplying both sides of this equation by $n = n_1 + n_2$ and dividing by 2, we obtain

$$\frac{n(U^2 - u^2)}{2} = n^2 pq - (n_1 + n_2)(n_1 p_1 q_1 + n_2 p_2 q_2)$$

and since $n^2 pq = np \cdot nq = (n_1 p_1 + n_2 p_2)(n_1 q_1 + n_2 q_2)$, we get

$$\frac{n(U^2 - u^2)}{2} = (n_1 p_1 + n_2 p_2)(n_1 q_1 + n_2 q_2) - (n_1 + n_2)(n_1 p_1 q_1 + n_2 p_2 q_2)$$

$$= n_1 n_2 (p_1 - p_2)(q_2 - q_1)$$

Finally, since $p_1 + q_1 = 1$ and $p_2 + q_2 = 1$ gives $q_2 - q_1 = p_1 - p_2$, we get

$$U^2 - u^2 = \frac{2 n_1 n_2}{n}(p_1 - p_2)^2$$

It can be seen from this result that if p_1 is different from p_2, that is, the two groups are really distinct, U^2 is always greater than u^2. In other words, the unit deviation is larger than it is in the case where there is only one kind of trial. This rule is confirmed immediately by the special case where one has $p_1 = 1$, $q_1 = 0$, $p_2 = 0$, and $q_2 = 1$; referring again to the example of the urns, we thus replace n drawings from an urn containing white and black balls in the ratio of p to q by $n_1 = np$ drawings from an urn containing only white balls and $n_2 = nq$ drawings from an urn containing only black balls. It is clear that under these conditions there could be no deviations (other than zero).

Let us now evaluate the relative variation of the unit deviation. To begin with, we have

$$\frac{U^2 - u^2}{U^2} = \frac{2 n_1 n_2}{2 n^2 pq}(p_1 - p_2)^2$$

and if we substitute $n_1 = k_1 n$ and $n_2 = (1 - k_1)n$, this becomes

$$\frac{U^2 - u^2}{U^2} = \frac{k_1(1 - k_1)}{p(1 - p)}(p_1 - p_2)^2$$

In the special case where k_1 and p are contained between 1/4 and 3/4, we have

$$\frac{3}{16} < k_1(1 - k_1) < \frac{1}{4} \quad \text{and} \quad \frac{3}{16} < p(1 - p) < \frac{1}{4}$$

so that the fraction $\dfrac{k_1(1 - k_1)}{p(1 - p)}$ is contained between 3/4 and 4/3. It is thus that the term $(p_1 - p_2)^2$ determines the order of magnitude of the ratio

$$\frac{U^2 - u^2}{U^2} = 1 - \frac{u^2}{U^2}$$

Suppose, for example, that one has $n_1 = n_2$, $p_1 = q_2$, $p_2 = q_1$, and hence $p = q = 1/2$. It follows that

$$\frac{U^2 - u^2}{U^2} = (p_1 - p_2)^2 = (1 - 2p_1)^2$$

and that

$$U^2 = \frac{u^2}{1 - (1 - 2p_1)^2} = \frac{u^2}{4p_1q_1}$$

since $p_2 = q_1 = 1 - p_1$. Assuming that $p_1 = 3/4$ and $p_2 = q_1 = 1/4$, one obtains

$$U^2 = \frac{4u^2}{3} \quad \text{and} \quad U = \frac{2u}{\sqrt{3}}$$

Thus, if instead of making drawings from a single urn containing as many white balls as black balls, one makes the same number of drawings alternately from one urn containing three times as many white balls as black balls and a second urn containing three times as many black balls as white balls, the unit deviation is multiplied by $2/\sqrt{3}$, or approximately 1.15. The importance of these considerations will become evident when we shall study the probabilities of causes.

5.7 Extension to Several Groups

We shall not go into any of the details of the analytical developments by which one can treat the case where there are several groups. Let us merely observe that one can combine several groups step by step, by first combining two groups into a single group, then combining this single group with a third group, and so on. The general rule will thus follow from the rule we have just established for the case of two groups. It may be stated as follows:

RULE. *Suppose that one performs μ groups of trials, n_1 of the first kind, n_2 of the second kind, . . . , and that the corresponding probabilities for successes and failures are $p_1, p_2, \ldots, p_\mu$, and $q_1, q_2, \ldots, q_\mu$, respectively. The unit deviation for the whole set of trials is given by the formula*

$$u^2 = u_1^2 + u_2^2 + \ldots + u_\mu^2$$

where $u_1^2 = 2n_1p_1q_1$, $u_2^2 = 2n_2p_2q_2$, . . . , and $u_\mu^2 = 2n_\mu p_\mu q_\mu$; in other words, u_1, $u_2, \ldots$, and u_μ are the unit deviations corresponding to the individual groups of trials.

If one designates by $n_1p_1 + n_2p_2 + \ldots + n_\mu p_\mu + \lambda u$ the total number of successes, the relative deviation λ follows the normal probability law; that is, the probability that it is contained between λ and $\lambda + d\lambda$ is

$$\frac{1}{\sqrt{\pi}} e^{-\lambda^2} d\lambda$$

Let us now look for the deviation U in the case where the μ groups of trials are replaced by a single group of n trials, and where the probabilities for a success and a failure are p and q, respectively. We thus have

$$n = n_1 + n_2 + \ldots + n_\mu, \qquad np = n_1 p_1 + n_2 p_2 + \ldots + n_\mu p_\mu$$

$$nq = n_1 q_1 + n_2 q_2 + \ldots + n_\mu q_\mu, \qquad nU^2 = 2n^2 pq = 2 \cdot np \cdot nq$$

and it follows that

$$\frac{n(U^2 - u^2)}{2} = \sum n_1 p_1 \cdot \sum n_1 q_1 - \sum n_1 \cdot \sum n_1 p_1 q_1$$

$$= \sum \sum n_i n_k p_i q_k - \sum \sum n_i n_k p_k q_i$$

$$= \sum \sum{}' n_i n_k (p_i - p_k)(q_k - q_i)$$

where $\sum'$ is meant to indicate that each product $n_i n_k$ is taken only once. That is, one does not consider $n_i n_k$ as well as $n_k n_i$.

Finally, one thus obtains

$$U^2 = u^2 + \frac{2}{n} \sum \sum{}' n_i n_k (p_i - p_k)^2$$

As should have been expected, the second term on the right-hand side can never be negative.

5.8 *Summary of Results*

To summarize, the study of a problem in discrete probability where the number of trials is so large that they cannot be completely enumerated, requires (1) knowledge of the probability law followed by the relative deviation λ, the one given by $\theta(\lambda)$, and (2) calculation of the unit deviation u. The probability that a deviation is contained between $\lambda_1 u$ and $\lambda_2 u$ equals the probability that λ is contained between λ_1 and λ_2; that is, assuming that λ_1 and λ_2 are positive and $\lambda_1 < \lambda_2$, it is given by

$$\frac{1}{2}[\theta(\lambda_2) - \theta(\lambda_1)]$$

which can be written as

$$\frac{1}{2\sqrt{\pi}} \int_{\lambda_1}^{\lambda_2} e^{-\lambda^2} \, d\lambda$$

Thus, putting $\lambda u = h$, $\lambda_1 u = h_1$, and $\lambda_2 u = h_2$, the integral becomes

$$\frac{1}{2u\sqrt{\pi}} \int_{h_1}^{h_2} e^{-h^2/u^2} \, dh$$

This is the probability that the absolute deviation h is contained between h_1 and h_2 (regardless of their signs, provided $h_2 - h_1$ is positive). For a single series of trials one has $u^2 = 2npq$ and the formula becomes

$$\frac{1}{2\sqrt{2\pi npq}} \int_{h_1}^{h_2} e^{-h^2/2npq} \, dh$$

However, since the evaluation of these expressions requires the use of the table of values of $\theta(\lambda)$, *it is better not to introduce the absolute deviation h and work instead with the relative deviation λ and its unit deviation u.*

CHAPTER SIX

The Law of Chance

6.1 *The Law of Chance*

The practical applications of the results of the preceding chapters are dominated by an empirical law which, as we shall see, must be regarded as absolutely certain; we shall call it *the law of chance*. This law can be stated quite simply in the following form: *Events whose probability is extremely small never occur*. It will be convenient, however, to amplify this statement and to indicate what one means by an extremely small probability; this is what we shall do presently.

We shall predicate from the start that if the probability of an event is not extremely small, knowledge of this probability can play an important role in making a decision, but it cannot force this decision upon us. For example, if we want to take a trip and we have the choice of going by car, train, boat, or plane, statistics tell us the respective probabilities of having a fatal accident. Knowledge of these probabilities might affect our decision, but it cannot force it upon us; certain advantages of comfort or speed might lead us to incur a risk, provided this risk appears to be sufficiently small.

In other situations it may be possible to calculate the mathematical expectation, say, of a lottery ticket or of a bet in roulette. Someone who enjoys playing the game might buy a ticket or make a bet even when the amount he can lose exceeds his expected gain.

We shall now try to account for the case where the probability is so small that it is practically negligible, allowing for the fact that we are human beings living on the earth, which itself is situated in the universe. We shall thus view the problem successively from the human perspective, the terrestrial perspective, and the cosmic perspective.

6.2 *The Human Perspective*

We all know from everyday experience that people ignore certain small probabilities, even though the corresponding events may be of great importance, say, a matter of life or death. Accident statistics for cities like Paris show that there is about one fatal traffic accident per day for each million inhabitants. We can thus accept one millionth as the probability that a Parisian who goes out into the street on a certain day will have a fatal accident. If Parisians did not neglect such a probability, they would refuse to go out and the life of the city would be paralyzed.

One can give many other examples to show that a probability equal to or less than 0.000001 is generally regarded as negligible from the human perspective. In spite of this, some people will buy lottery tickets to which they are attracted by the size of the grand prize, even though there may be millions of tickets. However, even in that kind of situation the lottery would have few clients unless it offered some second and third prizes; most sensible human beings will carefully consider their slim chances of winning the grand prize, if an enterprise requires a good deal of capital.

6.3 *The Terrestrial Perspective*

The number of human beings living on the earth is approximately two billion, and an accident whose probability is very small for an individual can nevertheless happen quite frequently. This happens, for example, in the spread of a contagious disease; the probability of catching the disease on a given day is very small for a given individual, but if we consider a country as a whole, it can happen often enough to justify the implementation of measures designed to suppress or at least diminish the risk of contagion.

Insurance companies, whose clients number in the hundreds of thousands or millions, account for this in establishing their rates, even though the risks may be very slight for each individual client.

If then, after having accepted a probability of 10^{-6} as negligible from the human perspective, we divide this figure by 10^9, we conclude that a probability less than 10^{-15} is negligible from the terrestrial perspective.

6.4 *The Cosmic Perspective*

To evaluate what probabilities are negligible from the cosmic perspective, that is, the perspective of our universe, one might assume an anthropocentric point of view, namely, one might imagine the universe in the image of our planet and our solar system. The star closest to the sun is at a distance of approximately three light years. If one estimates the dimension of the visible universe as three billion light years, one would have to agree that the number of stars in this universe is of the magnitude of a billion cubed, that is, 10^{27}, and that it would thus contain at most 10^{30} planets like the earth. A probability negligible from the cosmic perspective would thus be given by the quotient of the probability negligible from the terrestrial perspective divided by 10^{30}, which is 10^{-45}.

It is not necessary, however, to take such a naïve anthropocentric point of view. It would be more logical to turn our attention to natural phenomena which can occur in the universe, without having to compare them with phenomena requiring the existence of the human race on our planet. The smallest particles into which matter seems to be divided have a linear dimension greater than 10^{-40} times the billions of light years which represent the linear dimension of the universe. The number of these particles would be less than the cube of 10^{40}, or 10^{120}, even if they were assumed to occupy space without a void. On the other hand, the most elementary phenomenon such as the collision of two of the particles occurs (for a given particle) in an interval of time that is very small compared to a second. Nevertheless, fewer than 10^{40} such intervals elapse in the course of billions of centuries, so that the total number of these infinitely small elementary phenomena does not exceed 10^{160} in the entire universe and during the longest period of time we can assign to the duration of our solar system. It is thus impossible to imagine that the simplest event could recur more than 10^{160} times, and it follows that a probability of 10^{-200} is very largely negligible from the cosmic perspective. One can say with certainty that a phenomenon to which such a probability can be assigned has never been observed and will never be observed by any human in the entire universe.

6.5 *The Supercosmic Perspective*

The study of very elementary and very simple problems of probability can easily lead to the definition of probabilities much smaller than those negligible from the cosmic perspective. We shall say that such probabilities are negligible from the supercosmic perspective, and that the events corresponding to these probabilities may be regarded as rigorously impossible.

The probabilities we shall consider here are defined relative to books written in a language having an alphabet, and we shall refer to them as *alphabetical probabilities.*

Suppose that an urn contains a number of balls, one for each letter of the French alphabet (and, perhaps, also one for each punctuation sign or other symbol used in typography). From this urn one randomly draws one ball, notes the letter that is inscribed, returns the ball to the urn, mixes the balls, and repeats the same operation a great number of times. One thus obtains an arbitrarily large sequence of letters which are chosen at random. What is the probability that such a sequence reproduces a predetermined text, say, an Alexandrian verse, a tragedy by Racine, or the complete works of Victor Hugo? If, for the sake of simplicity, we limit ourselves to the 26 letters of the French alphabet and neglect all additional signs, we would have to draw the following 37 letters to obtain the first line of *Athalie*:

o u i j e v i e n s d a n s s o n t e m p l e a d o r e r l e t e r n e l

The probability that the first letter is an *o* is 1/26, the probability that the second letter is a *u* is 1/26, . . . , and the probability of obtaining the above sequence of letters is thus 26^{-37}, which is less than 10^{-50}. If, instead of considering a single line, we considered a poem of 1,000 lines, the corresponding probability would be less than $10^{-50,000}$. If one considers a library of a million volumes, where each volume contains on the average a million letters, the probability of reconstructing these volumes exactly by means of random drawings will be less than a power of ten whose negative exponent, in absolute value, exceeds a thousand billions. This is the probability of what I have called the "miracle of the dactylographic monkeys"; namely, the probability that thousands of monkeys, randomly typing on typewriters, reproduce exactly the entire National Library.

Everyone will surely agree that such a miracle is absolutely impossible. Nevertheless, men of science and mathematicians in particular are accustomed to distrust assertions based on judgment or common sense. They do not forget that during the course of time, even quite recently, common sense denied the existence of antipodes, or the movement of the earth around the sun. It is thus indispensable to examine what might be called the argument of the mathematician.

6.6 *The Argument of the Mathematician*

This argument is very simple and of a purely arithmetical nature. Let *p* be the probability of an event, where *p* is a nonzero positive number which can be very small. Given such a number *p*, how often must one repeat the experiment to be almost certain that the corresponding event will occur? If the experiment is repeated *n* times, the probability that the event will not occur even once is given by $P = (1 - p)^n$ according to the principle of composite probabilities. Furthermore, if *p* is very small one commits a negligible error if one replaces $1 - p$ with e^{-p}, and this gives

$$P = e^{-pn}$$

If the product *pn* is sufficiently large, say, 1,000, the probability *P* will be extremely small and there will be an almost absolute certainty that the event (whose probability is *p*) will occur at least once. It will thus suffice to repeat the experiment with the dactylographic monkeys *n* times to be practically certain that the "miracle" will occur at least once, that is, that the monkeys will reproduce, without a single mistake, all of the volumes of the National Library.

These calculations are incontestable, as are all calculations that do not entail any approximations. Nevertheless, it is not only contestable but absurd, if one tries to imagine the concrete significance of the abstract words in the phrase "it will suffice to repeat the experiment n times," when n equals a power of 10 whose exponent exceeds a thousand billions, namely, a number having more than a thousand billion digits. In fact, we have seen that if we turn our attention to the most elementary and the most simple of experiences which are by far the most frequent (such as collisions of infinitesimal particles, the ultimate elements of matter and energy), and we do so over an interval of time exceeding by far the life of our solar system, the number of times that an experiment can be repeated does not exceed a power of 10 whose exponent is less than a thousand. The innocent phrase "it will suffice to repeat . . ." is as ridiculous as it would be for a Christian to say, "It suffices to be God the Father."

Some philosophers will ask whether the universe is not really infinite; but if this is so, all of the most complicated combinations such as the arrangement of all the atoms which at this hour actually constitute the terrestrial sphere are not only possible, but are realized an infinite number of times even though their probability is very small compared to that of the miracle of the monkeys. But again, one must assume that in this universe which we try to imagine there exists a certain homogeneity, in the sense that the simple elements which constitute our universe are able to form the same combinations throughout the entire extent of the infinite universe. There is really no need to go into the unreasonableness of such an anthropocentric picture of an infinite universe. If we designate by U_1 our universe which extends as far as some billions of light years, and (according to Boltzmann) by U_2 a universe which compares to U_1 as U_1 compares to an atom, by U_3 a universe which compares to U_2 as U_2 compares to U_1, and so on, we would be forced to admit that we could never know anything about U_2 even if we knew U_1 perfectly. In particular, the hypothesis that U_2 is composed of a great number of elements analogous to U_1 is extremely improbable. All speculations concerning $U_2, U_3, \ldots$, and even more so concerning $U_{1,000}$ and $U_{1,000,000}$ are pure metaphysics and not science. Evidently, there is nothing to prevent a metaphysician from asking whether the particular combinations connected with what we call "life," which are undoubtedly very improbable, occur only a few times or if, though extremely rare, they occur infinitely often. Once one admits the concept of infinity, one might as well assert that infinity is sufficiently copious to make all this possible. Of course, this attitude is entirely contrary to the scientific spirit, which wants to gain knowledge about the universe as it is, and not as it could be.

6.7 Application to Repeated Trials

The application of the law of chance to the problem of repeated trials permits the derivation of certain results which are practically certain (from the human perspective) or even absolutely certain (from the cosmic perspective). We know that the probability that the absolute value of the relative deviation exceeds λ is $1 - \theta(\lambda)$, which is 10^{-12} for $\lambda = 5$ and of the order of 10^{-50} for $\lambda = 10$; for $\lambda = 4.06$ it is 10^{-8}. Thus, values of λ exceeding 4 are seldom observed and values of λ exceeding 5 are practically unobservable from the human and even from the terrestrial perspective. So far as values of λ exceeding 10 are concerned, they are impossible from the cosmic perspective.

Given 1,000,000 repeated trials for which $p = q = 1/2$, the unit deviation is $\sqrt{2npq} = \sqrt{500,000}$ or approximately 700. Thus, a deviation of 2,800 is very exceptional and a deviation of 3,500 is practically impossible; so far as a deviation of 7,000 is concerned, it must be considered as rigorously impossible. The number of successes will practically always be contained between 497,000 and 503,000, and it is absolutely certain that it will be contained between 490,000 and 510,000. Anticipating the theory of the probability of causes (Part III), one might conclude from this, for example, that since one has observed 51 per cent male births among millions of births, it is absolutely certain that the respective probabilities for male and female births are not equal; if they were equal, such a large deviation would be impossible.

The law of chance also clarifies the law of large numbers for all cases where the number of trials is fixed. The number of successes must certainly be contained between $np \pm 5\sqrt{2npq}$, and hence the proportion of successes must be contained between the limits $p \pm 5\sqrt{2pq/n}$. It must be added, however, that this result applies only to a series of well-determined trials; that is, the number n must be regarded as given and the n trials must actually be realizable (which would not be the case if n exceeded $10^{1,000}$). The study of an infinite sequence of repeated trials is a different matter; it is only of theoretical interest, since an infinite sequence of trials cannot possibly be realized. This is connected with the theory of denumerable probabilities, which we shall not be able to discuss in detail. Nevertheless, it will be appropriate to say a few words on this subject, because of the importance it has assumed in modern theoretical research in probability.

6.8 A Simple Problem of Denumerable Probabilities

The following is the simplest problem in the theory of denumerable probabilities: imagine an infinite sequence of repeated trials which are numbered 1, 2, ... (that is, there is a denumerable infinity of trials); the probability of a success in the nth trial is p_n. What is the probability that there will be infinitely many successes? The answer to this question is quite easily found and it depends only on the convergence or divergence of the series

(1) $$S = p_1 + p_2 + \ldots + p_n + \ldots$$

If the series S converges, one is said to be in the case of convergence, and the probability P that there will be infinitely many successes is equal to zero; if the series S diverges one is said to be in the case of divergence and the probability P is equal to 1.

Complete proofs of this may be found in other books. The abbreviated version we are going to give here is equally rigorous, however, at least for those who are familiar with the concept of mathematical expectation.

If the series (1) converges, its value is less than some integer a, and it may thus be decomposed into b partial sums (one of which is the sum of infinitely many terms), where each partial sum has a value less than a, and where b is an integer which may exceed a, but which is less than $2a$.

On the other hand, if the series (1) diverges, it can be decomposed into infinitely many partial sums, each of which has a value greater than 1.

Let us now concentrate on one of the partial sums

$$s = p_1 + p_2 + \ldots + p_k$$

whose value is less than 1 in the case of convergence and greater than 1 in the case of divergence. The mathematical expectation of a player who receives an amount equal to unity for each success in the k trials is evidently equal to s. It follows that there would have to be on the average less than 1 success when s is less than 1, and more than 1 success if s is greater than 1. Consequently, in the case of convergence a success will occur on the average at most b times, and in the case of divergence a success will occur on the average infinitely often. This is precisely the result we asserted above.

It is known that the boundary line between convergence and divergence cannot be given precisely by means of a denumerable infinity of criteria, but it is also known that the logarithmic criteria of Bertrand make it possible to form convergent and divergent series which are remarkably alike, at least for all the terms one can actually write.

To formulate such series, it will be convenient to designate by log x a number equal to the logarithm to the base 10 of x when x is greater than or equal to 10, but equal to 1 when x is less than 10. With this convention, the iterated logarithms

$$\log (\log x) = \log_2 x$$
$$\log (\log_2 x) = \log_3 x$$

are defined for all integral values of x and they are at least equal to 1.

Let us limit ourselves to the simplest criteria of Bertrand: the series

$$\sum \frac{1}{n \cdot \log n (\log_2 n)^2}$$

converges, whereas the series

$$\sum \frac{1}{n \cdot \log n \log_2 n}$$

diverges. However, if n is less than 10^{10} the corresponding terms of the two series are equal; after that they differ by a factor which decreases slowly and becomes equal to $1/2$ for $n = 10^{100}$ and equal to $1/3$ for $n = 10^{1,000}$.

It follows that the fundamental theorem of the theory of denumerable probabilities, whose theoretical importance is very great, is without interest from a practical point of view. One can actually construct a convergent series having each term less than 1 but a value exceeding a power of 10 whose exponent has a billion digits, and a divergent series for which one obtains a sum less than 1 for a number of terms equalling a power of 10 whose exponent has a billion digits. In the first case, the number of successes will exceed one's imagination even though there is convergence; in the second case, it would be practically impossible to observe more than one success even though there is divergence. These practical observations do not diminish the interest of the application of the fundamental theorem to the theory of repeated trials.

6.9 Application of the Theory of Denumerable Probabilities to the Theory of Repeated Trials

Let us consider an unlimited sequence of repeated trials and let us designate by p_n the probability that at the nth trial the relative deviation λ exceeds a given number λ_n. This probability is

$$(2) \qquad p_n = 1 - \theta(\lambda_n) = \frac{2}{\sqrt{\pi}} \int_{\lambda_n}^{\infty} e^{-\lambda^2} \, d\lambda$$

It is clear that if the numbers λ_n are constants, so are the probabilities p_n. Thus, no matter how large λ_n might be and, hence, no matter how small p_n might be, the series p_n will diverge and one can assert that there will be infinitely many successes (where the relative deviation exceeds the corresponding constant λ_n).

It can be seen that, in appearance, this result contradicts those we stated in Section 6.7. Nevertheless, it is correct that if one gives λ_n a fixed value greater than 10, the constant value of p_n is of the order of magnitude of 10^{-50} and, hence, the case which we have referred to as favorable will never happen. In other words, one will not observe a relative deviation greater than λ_n. So far as even greater, though still constant, values of λ_n are concerned, a deviation exceeding λ_n would be as improbable as the miracle of the dactylographic monkeys. Of course, a mathematician might object that he is certain to observe such a deviation if the experiment is repeated a sufficiently large number of times (just as it suffices to repeat the experiment with the monkeys sufficiently often to assure a success). As we have seen, this objection has no practical significance whatsoever.

It is nevertheless quite interesting from the theoretical point of view to determine λ_n as a function of n such that the series p_n will converge. According to (2) one evidently has

$$(3) \qquad p_n < A \cdot e^{-\lambda_n^2}$$

where A is a numerical constant whose value does not matter. If one puts

(4) $$\lambda_n = \sqrt{2 \cdot \log n}$$

where log designates the Naperian logarithm, formula (3) gives

(5) $$p_n < \frac{A}{n^2}$$

and we find ourselves well in the case of convergence. One can thus assert that the probability for infinitely many successes is equal to zero; this kind of success can occur only a finite number of times.* In any case, one can assert that beginning with a certain value of n, the relative deviation will be less than $\sqrt{2 \cdot \log n}$, which goes to say that in a series of n repeated trials with the constant probability $p = 1 - q$, the number of successes will definitely be contained in the interval

(6) $$np \pm \sqrt{2 \cdot \log n} \sqrt{2npq}$$

starting with some value of n. Correspondingly, the proportion of successes will be contained in the interval

(7) $$p \pm \frac{2\sqrt{pq \cdot \log n}}{\sqrt{n}}$$

where log designates the Naperian logarithm.

Formula (7) expresses the fact which Kolmogorov and other mathematicians have called the *strong law of large numbers*. It can be seen that it is an immediate consequence of the fundamental theorem of the theory of denumerable probabilities.

6.10 *Conclusion*

It can be seen that the domain of applicability of the law which we have referred to as the law of chance is very large; the law covers practically all problems of discrete probabilities one can effectively pose.

At times, the theory of denumerable probabilities seems to conflict with the law of chance, but one must never forget that it is a purely mathematical theory, and that it has no practical basis since it assumes the realization of a denumerable infinity of trials. At the end of Part II, which is devoted to continuous probabilities, we shall see that such a denumerable infinity of trials is equivalent to the choice of an element (a point) in a continuous set. This presents another point of view, from which one can view the theory of denumerable probabilities and, as a consequence, the law of chance.

---

* Using the reasoning based on mathematical expectations employed in Section 6.8, it can easily be shown that this finite number is certainly very small.

PART TWO

Continuous Probabilities

CHAPTER SEVEN

Definition of Geometrical Probability

7.1 *Position of a Point on a Line*

Let us consider a line segment AB and a point M which must lie on AB (see Figure 1). What is the probability that M will occupy a given position on AB? This question is different from those studied in Part I, inasmuch as the number of possibilities is infinite, since M can vary continuously between A and B. This makes it necessary to give a new definition of probability. Any such definition is, of course, only a mathematical convention, but it is not an *arbitrary* convention; it suggests itself *a priori* through the study of various questions, and it is verified *a posteriori* by the agreement between its consequences and observations. When a mathematican says that something is a convention, this merely goes to say that since he cannot demonstrate it rigorously, he prefers to consider it as a convention and, thus, make his reasoning unassailable. The problem of justifying the convention is thus transferred to each individual concrete example.

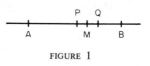

FIGURE 1

DEFINITION. *The probability that the point M falls on any given segment PQ of AB is proportional to the length of PQ.**

CONSEQUENCE. *If M is assumed to lie on AB, the probability that it falls on*

---

* Here and in what follows we shall consider segments from the point of view of their arithmetic measure, and not their algebraic value; in other words, we do consider their signs.

AB is equal to 1 and, hence, the probability that it falls on PQ is equal to PQ/AB.

It should be noted that this definition and its consequences are not beyond criticism. One could exhibit these difficulties geometrically making use of a homographic transformation (or conical projection), but we shall exhibit them algebraically.

7.2 *An Objection to the Definition*

If a number x must be contained between 5 and 10, it follows from the preceding that its probability of falling between 5 and 6 is given by

$$\frac{6-5}{10-5} = \frac{1}{5}$$

On the other hand, if we consider the square of x, where x is contained between 5 and 10, then x^2 is contained between 25 and 100, and if x is contained between 5 and 6, x^2 is contained between 25 and 36. Thus, the probability that x^2 is contained between 25 and 36, given that it must fall between 25 and 100, is given by

$$\frac{36-25}{100-25} = \frac{11}{75}$$

Now let us consider $1/x$. If x is contained between 5 and 10 or between 5 and 6, then $1/x$ must be contained, respectively, between 1/5 and 1/10 or between 1/5 and 1/6. Hence, the probability that $1/x$ is contained between 1/5 and 1/6, given that it must fall between 1/5 and 1/10, is given by

$$\frac{1/5 - 1/6}{1/5 - 1/10} = \frac{1/30}{1/10} = \frac{1}{3}$$

This would seem to prove that the definition is inacceptable for, clearly, it is absurd to obtain different results if one replaces x by a simple function of x. More generally, if $f(x)$ is an arbitrary monotonic function of x on the interval from a to b, the probability that x falls between c and d, where $a < c < d < b$, is given by

$$P = \frac{f(d) - f(c)}{f(b) - f(a)}$$

since this is the probability that $f(x)$ is contained between $f(c)$ and $f(d)$. Appropriately choosing $f(x)$, one can thus assign P any arbitrary value between 0 and 1. This is the objection which we have given with all its force, but whose practical significance is not very great.

Later on, we shall treat some of the questions posed from a theoretical point of view; we shall do so in connection with some remarks made by

Poincaré to the effect that under certain conditions the final result is independent of the choice of the arbitrary function $f(x)$. For the time being, let us remain on concrete ground.

From the practical point of view, the preceding objection simply draws our attention to the fact that errors can be made through an erroneous choice of the independent variable. In reality, this choice is almost always dictated in an obvious manner by the conditions of the questions posed, regardless of whether such questions are abstract or concrete. Hence, it is simply a pleasantry to pretend that this choice can be modified arbitrarily by a change of variable, which is nothing but an analytic artifact with no bearing upon reality. In Chapter 8 we shall give an exact account of the manner in which the independent variable must be chosen in certain special problems, but this choice makes no sense unless it pertains to problems formulated in such a way that an experimental verification can at least be attempted (see the beginning of Chapter 8).*

7.3 *Position of a Point in the Plane or in Space*

If a point M must be contained in a plane region A, the probability that it falls into some specified part S of A is proportional to the area of S; that is, it equals the ratio S/A, where S and A designate the areas of the corresponding regions (see Fig. 2). Analytically, this probability is expressed by the ratio

$$\frac{\displaystyle\iint_S dx\, dy}{\displaystyle\iint_A dx\, dy}$$

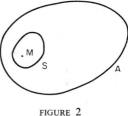

FIGURE 2

If the point M must be in the interior of some solid V, the probability that it falls into a portion U of this solid is equal to U/V, and it may be calculated by means of the ratio

$$\frac{\displaystyle\iiint_U dx\, dy\, dz}{\displaystyle\iiint_V dx\, dy\, dz}$$

These expressions make it possible to calculate the expected value of an arbitrary function $f(x, y, z)$; it equals the sum of the products obtained by multiplying each possible value of the function by its probability, that is to

---

* Readers who are interested mainly in applications can omit the remainder of this chapter and go on directly to the problems of Chapter 8.

say, it is given by

$$\frac{\iiint_V f(x, y, z) \, dx \, dy \, dz}{\iiint_V dx \, dy \, dz}$$

Using the language of the geometry of n dimensions, one can extend these definitions and these results to the case where the number of independent variables exceeds 3; this is often done in mathematical physics (see Chapter 9).

7.4 *Other Geometrical Probabilities*

Sometimes one must consider probabilities which do not pertain to the position of a point, but to some other geometrical element depending on one or more variables. The choice of the variables may be very simple and follow directly from the formulation of the problem, or it may be quite complicated. It is in the treatment of special problems (Chapter 8) that one can best account for the difficulties that present themselves and the steps one must follow to surmount them. For the moment, let us give some general indications.

Let us first consider the case where a point must lie on a curve in a plane or on a surface in space. Most common among these problems are those where a point must lie on a circle or on a sphere, in which case it would seem natural to consider probabilities as being proportional to the length of the arc or to the area of the spherical surface. An analogous problem arises when a line must pass through a fixed point in the plane or in space, and one considers its intersection with a circle or a sphere having the fixed point as its center. In the plane, the position of the line would be determined by the angle φ it makes with a given direction, where φ varies from 0 to π if the line is looked upon as extending indefinitely in both directions, or from 0 to 2π if the line is looked upon as a ray. Taking the latter case, the probability that the angle between the ray and the fixed direction falls between φ_1 and φ_2 $(0 < \varphi_1 < \varphi_2 < 2\pi)$ is given by

$$\frac{\varphi_2 - \varphi_1}{2\pi} = \frac{\displaystyle\int_{\varphi_1}^{\varphi_2} d\varphi}{\displaystyle\int_0^{2\pi} d\varphi}$$

and the probable (or mean) value of a function $f(\varphi)$ is given by

$$\frac{1}{2\pi} \int_0^{2\pi} f(\varphi) \, d\varphi$$

In order to determine the position of a point on a sphere (or the direction of a ray in space) one must use two coordinates, which may be the longitude

θ varying from $-\pi$ to π and the latitude φ varying from $-\pi/2$ to $\pi/2$. The coordinates of a point on the sphere are thus given by

$$x = R \cdot \cos \theta \cdot \cos \varphi$$
$$y = R \cdot \sin \theta \cdot \cos \varphi$$
$$z = R \cdot \sin \varphi$$

where θ varies from $-\pi$ to π and φ varies from $-\pi/2$ to $\pi/2$. The element of surface area is $R^2 \cdot \cos \varphi \cdot d\theta \, d\varphi$, so that the total surface area is

$$\int_{-\pi}^{\pi} d\theta \int_{-\pi/2}^{\pi/2} R^2 \cdot \cos \varphi \cdot d\varphi = 4\pi R^2$$

The probability that the direction of a ray is contained between certain limits is thus given by

$$\frac{1}{4\pi} \iint_{(s)} \cos \varphi \cdot d\theta \, d\varphi$$

where the double integral extends over the domain of variation (s) of the angles θ and φ. Similarly, the mean value of a function $f(\theta, \varphi)$ is given by

$$\frac{1}{4\pi} \int_{-\pi}^{\pi} \int_{-\pi/2}^{\pi/2} f(\theta, \varphi) \cos \varphi \cdot d\theta \, d\varphi$$

The preceding cases are the ones that arise most often; in the next chapter we shall discuss some special examples.

CHAPTER EIGHT

Some Problems of Geometrical Probabilities

8.1 *Preliminary Remarks*

Setting aside for the moment the general considerations developed in the preceding chapter, we shall now devote ourselves to the study of concrete problems of geometrical probabilities. By concrete problems we mean those for which the formulation is sufficiently precise so that one can deduce a method of experimental verification for the results. It will undoubtedly seem strange to some that there can be a question of *experimental verification* when there is an element of chance; if one wanted to verify experimentally the results one should get in the game of heads or tails, according to the rules of probability, would it not be possible to stumble on an unusual series of 1,000 consecutive heads? Would one conclude from this that the theory is false? Certainly not, but if one repeats the experiment a sufficient number of times, most of them will yield results that agree with the theory. An event such as the appearance of 1,000 consecutive heads in the game of heads or tails is as improbable as the following: a good physicist, using excellent instruments, measures the acceleration due to gravity by a new method and he obtains a value quite different from the one generally accepted. His first idea would be to repeat the experiment, and it would be only after numerous trials that he would gain faith in his results and search for the cause of the discrepancy elsewhere than in a random error.*

---

* A skeptic might say that in this way one does not count an experiment unless it confirms the provisions of the theory. Not at all, but the agreement of the results with prior experience is a reason to suppose that one has not stumbled on one of those gross errors which are the results of rare coincidences when the experimenter is competent and the instruments are thoroughly checked. Such coincidences are as rare as abnormal sequences in the game of heads or tails.

Nevertheless, it is not by means of a single verification, namely, a single series of experiments, that one tries to control the value of a geometrical probability. One must perform numerous series and if (except for some exceptional series) they give results that are close to the theoretical results, this constitutes support for the theory. One can use this method also to decide the following point: if two methods used in the theoretical study of a problem lead to entirely different results, experience will make it possible to eliminate one of the results with a certain degree of confidence and, hence, condemn one of the methods.

8.2 A Difficulty of Experimental Verification

In the experimental verification of results concerning geometrical probabilities there is one difficulty which cannot be ignored as it is of sufficient generality and, in some instances, has a bearing on the basic nature of things.

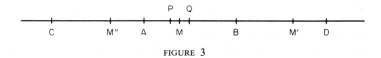

FIGURE 3

Let us consider the simplest case where one wants to determine the probability that a point M falls on a certain portion PQ of a line segment AB (see Figure 3). If one wants to determine this probability experimentally, one takes a real segment AB and attempts to put M on this segment in a random fashion. Thus, the segment AB could be a wooden ruler on which one throws "at random" a very small metallic object representing the point M. The difficulty which thus presents itself is the following: if it is desired in each case that the point M must fall on AB, one would have to aim more or less for the middle of AB and, without the need for any theory, common sense would indicate that the probability of M falling on a segment PQ (of a given length) would be greater when PQ is located near the middle of AB rather than near its extremes. One could treat the problem from this point of view with the methods of the theory of errors, but this would be a difficult problem whose usefulness is outweighed by the complications. We shall disregard this point of view completely; that is, we shall not assume that one strives to put M on AB. Thus, it can frequently happen that M will fall on the extension of AB, to the left or to the right, at M' or M''. One could disregard these positions of M, or one could consider the segments CA and BD (to the left and to the right of AB in Figure 3) and agree to represent each position of M on CA, for example, by the homological image on AB, namely, the position M'' would occupy if CA were superimposed on AB, with C on A and A on B. However, some reflection will show that this way of proceeding is not legitimate when the segments equal to AB

are very numerous, that is, if each of them is small compared to the variations of the position of M. In that case one would have a series of equal segments A_4A_3, A_3A_2, A_2A_1, A_1A, AB, BB_1, etc. (see Figure 4), all considered as homologous, and one would consider each position on one of them as equivalent to a homologous position on AB. This special form of interpreting an experiment is never required by the nature of things, but it can be useful in some instances (see, for example, the needle problem of Section 8.7). What

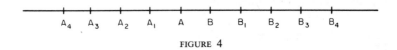

FIGURE 4

is essential is not to strain oneself to put M on AB as often as possible, so as not to violate the conditions of the problem.

8.3 *Problems Concerning the Position of a Point on a Line*

PROBLEM 22. *Two points M and M' are to be selected at random on a line segment of length l; what is the probability that the distance MM' is less than kl, where $k < 1$?*

If we designate by x the distance AM, the probability that this distance is contained between x and $x + dx$ is dx/l. If we now choose C and D so that $MC = MD = kl$, then MM' is less than kl if and only if M' is contained between C and D (see Figure 5.) However, since M' must also lie

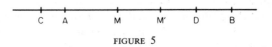

FIGURE 5

between A and B, one must distinguish between several cases depending on the relative positions of the points C, A, D, and B. When CD equals $2kl$, it is less than or greater than AB depending on whether k is less than or greater than $1/2$. We shall examine these cases separately, with each case subdivided further into the three possibilities listed below.

Order of the points	Inequality for x when $k < \frac{1}{2}$	Length of segment which must contain M'
$C\,A\,D\,B$	$0 < x < kl$	$AD = x + kl$
$A\,C\,D\,B$	$kl < x < (1-k)l$	$CD = 2kl$
$A\,C\,B\,D$	$(1-k)l < x < l$	$CB = kl + l - x$

For $k < 1/2$ the desired probability is thus

$$\frac{1}{l}\left[\int_0^{kl}(x+kl)\frac{dx}{l}+\int_{kl}^{(1-k)l}2kl\frac{dx}{l}+\int_{(1-k)l}^l(kl+l-x)\frac{dx}{l}\right]$$

and for $k > 1/2$ it is

$$\frac{1}{l}\left[\int_0^{(1-k)l}(x+kl)\frac{dx}{l}+\int_{(1-k)l}^{kl}l\cdot\frac{dx}{l}+\int_{kl}^l(kl+l-x)\frac{dx}{l}\right]$$

The calculations may be simplified if one observes that, for reasons of

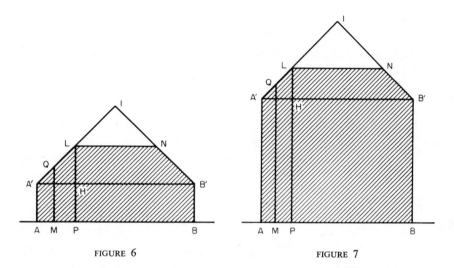

FIGURE 6   FIGURE 7

symmetry, the third integral in each of these formulas equals the first. Thus, for $k < 1/2$ one obtains

$$2\left[\frac{k^2}{2}+k^2\right]+2k(1-2k)=2k-k^2$$

and for $k > 1/2$ one obtains

$$2\left[\frac{(1-k)^2}{2}+k(1-k)\right]+2k-1=2k-k^2$$

The result is the same in either case, and it can be obtained more easily by evaluating areas rather than the integrals. Erecting for any point M on $AB = l$ (see Figures 6 and 7) an ordinate MQ equal in length to the segment which must contain M' when M is at the foot of the ordinate, one obtains a shaded area which, divided by l^2, gives the desired probability. Corresponding to $k < 1/2$ (Figure 6) one has

$$AA' = lk, \quad A'H = HL = kl, \quad PL = 2kl, \quad LN = l(1-2k)$$

and corresponding to $k > 1/2$ (Figure 7) one has

$$AA' = kl, \quad A'H = HL = (1 - k)l, \quad PL = l, \quad LN = l(2k - 1)$$

In both figures, the shaded area equals the rectangle $AA'B'B$ + the triangle $A'B'I$ — the triangle LNI, namely,

$$AB \cdot AA' + \frac{1}{4}(A'B')^2 - \frac{1}{4}(LN)^2$$

However, since LN equals $\pm l(1 - 2k)$, one has

$$AB \cdot AA' = l^2k$$
$$(A'B')^2 = l^2$$
$$(LN)^2 = l^2(1 - 2k)^2$$

for both figures, and the probability (obtained by dividing the shaded area by l^2) is thus

$$k + \frac{1 - (1 - 2k)^2}{4} = 2k - k^2$$

The following is another way of arriving at the same result: letting $AM = x$ and $AM' = y$, the probability that AM is contained between x and $x + dx$ and M' is contained between y and $y + dy$ is equal to $dx\,dy/l^2$. Representing the point P by its rectangular coordinates x and y (see Figure 8), we find that this point must be inside the square $OABC$ of side l, and the probability that it will fall in a given region must be proportional to its area. The condition imposed by the problem is that $|x - y| < kl$, which requires that P must be contained between the lines DE and FG, parallel to OB, whose equations are

$$x - y = \pm kl$$

The desired probability is thus equal to the ratio of the area of $ODEBGFO$ to the area of the square, and since the two right triangles ADE and CFG form a square of side $(1 - k)l$, since $OD = OF = kl$, it equals

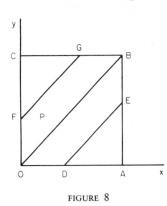

FIGURE 8

$$\frac{l^2 - (1 - k)^2 l^2}{l^2} = 2k - k^2$$

As should have been expected, the probability increases when k varies from 0 to 1; for $k = 0$ it equals 0, for $k = 1$ it equals 1, and for $k = 1/2$ it equals 3/4.

PROBLEM 23. *Two points M and M' are randomly selected on a segment AB of length l. What is the expected value of the distance MM' and that of its square?*

The solution of this problem can be deduced from results previously obtained. As it is known that the probability of MM' being less than kl is $2k - k^2$, the probability of MM' being contained between kl and $(k + dk)l$ equals the differential of $2k - k^2$, namely, $2(1 - k) \, dk$. Hence, the expected value of MM' is given by

$$\int_0^1 2(1 - k)kl \, dk = \frac{l}{3}$$

or $AB/3$ and the expected value of its square is given by

$$\int_0^1 2(1 - k)k^2l^2 \, dk = \frac{l^2}{6}$$

or $(AB)^2/6$. Note that the expected value of the square is greater than the square of the expected value.

To treat the problem directly, let us put $AM = x$, $AM' = y$, so that the expected value of MM' is given by

$$\frac{1}{l^2} \int_0^l \int_0^l |x - y| \, dx \, dy$$

since $MM' = |x - y|$. Now, one evidently has

$$\int_0^l |x - y| \, dx = \int_0^y (y - x) \, dx + \int_y^l (x - y) \, dx$$

$$= \frac{l^2}{2} - ly + y^2$$

and hence

$$\int_0^l \left(\frac{l^2}{2} - ly + y^2 \right) dy = \frac{l^3}{3}$$

so that the expected value is $l/3$.

So far as the expected value of $(MM')^2$ is concerned, one has

$$\frac{1}{l^2} \int_0^l \int_0^l (x - y)^2 \, dx \, dy = \frac{1}{l^2} \int_0^l \frac{(l - y)^3 + y^3}{3} \, dy = \frac{l^2}{6}$$

and, similarly, for the expected value of $(MM')^{2n}$ one has

$$\frac{1}{l^2} \int_0^l \int_0^l (x - y)^{2n} \, dx \, dy = \frac{1}{l^2} \int_0^l \frac{(l - y)^{2n+1} + y^{2n+1}}{2n + 1} \, dy$$

$$= \frac{2l^n}{(2n + 1)(2n + 2)}$$

8.4 *Problems Concerning the Position of a Point on a Circle*

PROBLEM 24. *Two points M and M' are randomly selected on the circumference of a circle. What is the probability that the smaller of the two arcs MM' is less than* α, *where* α < π?

This problem is easier than the preceding one, since one can arbitrarily fix the position of M without affecting the probability. Thus, M' must fall on an arc of length 2α whose midpoint is at M, and the desired probability is

$$\frac{2\alpha}{2\pi} = \frac{\alpha}{\pi}$$

The probability that MM' is contained between α and α + dα is thus dα/π, and the expected value of MM' is given by

$$\int_0^\pi \frac{\alpha}{\pi}\, d\alpha = \frac{\pi}{2}$$

PROBLEM 25. *If n points M_1, M_2, . . . , and M_n are randomly selected on the circumference of a circle, what is the expectation of a player who is to receive as many dollars as there are arcs $M_i M_k$ less than* α?

We have already seen that the probability that one of the arcs is less than α is α/π. Thus, if there are n points the number of combinations (of n objects taken two at a time) is $\frac{n(n-1)}{2}$, and the mathematical expectation is $\frac{n(n-1)\alpha}{2\pi}$. If one assumes that α equals one degree and if one lets n = 25, this expression becomes $\frac{25 \cdot 24}{2} \cdot \frac{1}{180} = \frac{5}{3}$.

The mathematical expectation is greater than one, although the *probability* that at least one of the arcs is less than one degree is less than one. This is accounted for by the fact that the player will receive an appreciable amount (perhaps as much as 300 dollars) when many of the arcs $M_i M_k$ are less than one degree.

8.5 *Problems Concerning the Position of Points in a Plane Region*

PROBLEM 26. *Two points M and M' are randomly selected inside a square of side a. What is the expected value of the square of the distance MM'?*

Designating the coordinates of M by x and y, and those of M' by x' and y', we have only to evaluate the following multiple integral

$$\frac{1}{a^4} \int_0^a \int_0^a \int_0^a \int_0^a [(x-x')^2 + (y-y')^2]\, dx\, dx'\, dy\, dy'$$

In successive steps one obtains

$$\int_0^a [(x - x')^2 + (y - y')^2]\, dx = \frac{(a - x')^3 + x'^3}{3} + a(y - y')^2$$

$$\int_0^a \left[\frac{(a - x')^3 + x'^3}{3} + a(y - y')^2 \right] dx' = \frac{a^4}{6} + a^2(y - y')^2$$

$$\int_0^a \int_0^a \left[\frac{a^4}{6} + a^2(y - y')^2 \right] dy\, dy' = \frac{a^6}{3}$$

and the desired mean value is $a^2/3$.

8.6 *Problems Concerning the Position of Points on a Sphere*

These problems are of special importance for, as we shall see in Part III, they tie in with various questions concerning the distribution of stars on the celestial sphere.

PROBLEM 27. *Two points M and M' are selected at random on the surface of a sphere. What is the probability that the smaller of the great circles MM' is less than* α?

This probability is the same regardless of the position of M and, hence, if M is fixed M' must fall on the curved surface of the segment which corresponds to a semicentral angle $MOA = \alpha$ (see Figure 9). Designating the radius of the sphere by R, one thus has $MP = OM - OP = R(1 - \cos \alpha)$, and the ratio of the area of the curved surface of the segment to the area of the sphere is

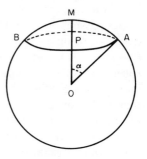

FIGURE 9

$$\frac{MP}{2R} = \frac{1 - \cos \alpha}{2} = \sin^2 \frac{\alpha}{2}$$

This is the desired probability. If α is very small one can replace $\sin \alpha/2$ by $\alpha/2$ and approximate the probability by $\alpha^2/4$.

In connection with the method just presented, Bertrand indicated an alternate kind of reasoning which leads to an entirely different result. Given two points M and M', the great circle joining them is determined, and since all great circles on the surface of a sphere are equivalent, the probability is not affected if one fixes the great circle in advance. As we have already seen, the probability that two points on a circle are such that MM' is less than α equals α/π, and this differs from the result obtained before, especially if α is very small. If α is 1 degree (or $\pi/180$ radians) one has

$$\frac{\alpha^2}{4} = \frac{\pi^2}{360^2} \quad \text{and} \quad \frac{\alpha}{\pi} = \frac{1}{180}$$

The ratio of the second value to the first is $720/\pi$, which is greater than 200. Must one conclude (as Bertrand did) that this problem cannot be resolved and that the first solution we gave is incorrect? To the contrary, this solution is the only correct one if one accepts the postulate relative to the elementary probabilities, namely, if one accepts that equal portions of the sphere are equiprobable so far as the location of M and M' is concerned. In the second way of reasoning Bertrand seems to be accepting this kind of *homogeneity*, if one can say that all points on the sphere may be looked upon as equivalent. However, this conceals a cause of inexactness which is worth examining and which we shall study closer.

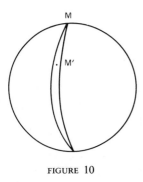

FIGURE 10

Let us begin by affirming that the probability is not changed if one fixes the arc of the great circle on which M and M' must lie as well as the position of M on this great circle; this is clear for reasons of symmetry. The error begins when (after the great circle and M are fixed) one assumes that the probability of M' falling on a given arc of the great circle is proportional to the length of the arc. If the arc of the great circle has no thickness one must, rigorously speaking, assign a zero probability to the event that M and M' both fall on the circle. In order to avoid this factor of zero which makes all calculations impossible, one must consider a thin bundle of arcs of great circles passing through M and it can then be seen that M' has greater probability of being a quadrant away from M than of lying in the vicinity of M (see Figure 10). Let us suppose, for example, that the sphere is the terrestrial sphere, M is the north pole, and M' is the point of impact of an aerolite put into space according to an unknown law with a velocity much greater than that of the earth. Now we may want to know the probability that the point of impact M' has a latitude greater than 89° North. Returning to the reasoning of Bertrand, one can say that the longitude of the point of impact is known (for example, one might assume that M' must lie on the meridian of Paris) and that all points on this meridian are equiprobable. As we shall see, however, even this point of view leads one to conclude that all the points on the meridian are *not* equiprobable through experimental verification. In fact, how does one verify that a point M' is on the meridian of Paris? If one determines its longitude with the aid of astronomical observations and a chronometer, this determination is made with a certain angular precision. Let us suppose, for example, that this precision is 0.1″; in other words, one considers not only the ideal line without thickness which would be the theoretical meridian, but the space contained between a longitude of 0.1″ East and a longitude of 0.1″ West. This space is greater at the equator than in the neighborhood of one of the poles, and the probability that the latitude of M' is contained between 0° and 1° East is thus much greater than the probability that it is contained between 89° and 90°.

One might think that the preceding reasoning can be refuted by substituting geodesic measurements for the astronomical observations. Let us suppose thus that one has drawn a meridian on the surface of the earth with very precise measurements; at least one might have determined a number of benchmarks, so that at least two of them can be seen from any point of the meridian. Let us also suppose that on each of these benchmarks there is a thin vertical stick to indicate its intersection with the plane of the meridian. If the center of gravity M' of the aerolite fell on the meridian thus defined, wouldn't the probability be the same at the equator and at the pole? Yes, undoubtedly, provided the vertical sticks placed on the benchmarks are all of the same thickness, but such a uniformity contradicts the notion of a meridian. No matter what thickness one might choose for the stick put on the benchmark located at the equator (say, for example, a tenth of a millimeter), the two edges of the stick actually define two meridians, whose angle is undoubtedly very small, since their separation at the equator is only a tenth of a millimeter; the separation becomes even smaller when one approaches a pole. If one placed two vertical sticks close together at the equator, each having a thickness of a tenth of a millimeter, so that the right-hand side of one coincided with the left-hand side of the other, it would be impossible to do the same thing when approaching a pole. Sooner or later the sticks would encroach upon each other, so that in the vicinity of the poles one would have no right to say that they were on one or the other of the meridians defined at the equator. This somewhat lengthy discussion was needed to put Bertrand's argument in the right light; it also illustrates why one must be on guard against inexact reasoning.

PROBLEM 28. *If n points are randomly selected on the surface of a sphere, what is the mathematical expectation of a person who is to receive a dollar for each pair of points whose angular distance is less than α?*

When α is small, the probability for each pair is essentially equal to $\alpha^2/4$ and, hence, the mathematical expectation is

$$\frac{n(n-1)}{2} \cdot \frac{\alpha^2}{4} = \frac{n(n-1)\alpha^2}{8}$$

This result is of importance in the study of the probability of causes (see Section 13.4).

8.7 *Further Problems*

PROBLEM 29 (THE NEEDLE PROBLEM). *If equidistant parallel lines are traced on a piece of paper on which a perfectly cylindrical needle is tossed at random, what is the probability that the needle will cross one of the parallel lines?*

This is a famous problem which has been known for a long time. It readily lends itself to experimental verification, which, in fact, has often been tried. Let us designate by $2a$ the distance between the parallel lines AB

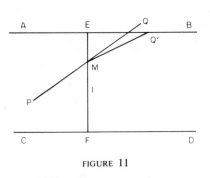

FIGURE 11

and CD and by $2l$ the length of the needle. It can be assumed that the midpoint M of the needle lies on a certain perpendicular EF to the parallel lines AB and CD. Let us designate by x the distance EM, supposedly less than FM, and let us suppose that $l < a$, namely, that the needle can cross at most one of the parallel lines. We shall see later that if it can cross several of the lines, one must, in order to arrive at a simple result, look for the mathematical expectation of a person who receives as many dollars as there are intersections rather than for the corresponding probability.

If the needle is to cross AB, x must be less than l, and if one designates by I the midpoint of EF, it is clear that the probability for EM to be contained between x and $x + dx$ (M being on EI) is dx/a. With M being fixed, it is necessary that the acute angle EMQ is less than the angle EMQ', where Q' lies on AB and $MQ = MQ'$. Thus, one has

$$\cos EMQ' = \frac{EM}{MQ'}$$

namely,

$$EMQ' = \text{arc cos } \frac{x}{l}$$

The probability that the angle EMQ (contained between 0 and $\pi/2$) is less than angle EMQ' is

$$\frac{2}{\pi} \text{ arc cos } \frac{x}{l}$$

and it follows that the probability of the needle crossing AB is

$$\frac{2}{\pi} \int_0^l \text{arc cos } \frac{x}{l} \frac{dx}{a}$$

Letting $x = ly$, this integral becomes

$$\frac{2l}{a\pi} \int_0^1 \text{arc cos } y \, dy$$

and the desired probability equals $a\pi/2l$, since the integral equals 1. To verify this one has only to put $y = \cos t$ and one obtains

$$\int_0^1 \text{arc cos } y \, dy = \int_{\pi/2}^0 -t \cdot \sin t \, dt = (t \cdot \cos t - \sin t)_{\pi/2}^0 = 1$$

In particular, if one assumes that $2l = a$, namely, that the length of the needle is half the distance between the parallel lines, the probability becomes equal to $1/\pi$. Thus, if one performs a sufficient number of trials, one obtains an approximation of the value of π. This has been tried many times and it has given perfectly satisfactory results, as satisfactory as it would be to estimate the ratio by means of drawings from an urn containing 314,159,265 balls of which 214,159,265 are black and 100,000,000 are white. For 4,000 trials the unit deviation is obtained by putting $n = 4,000$, $p = 1/\pi$, and $q = (\pi - 1)/\pi$, and one gets

$$\sqrt{2npq} = \frac{\sqrt{8,000(\pi - 1)}}{\pi}$$

which is a little greater than 10. Supposing that the value is 10, the error for $1/\pi$ would be in the neighborhood of $1/400$ and the error for π would be in the neighborhood of $1/100$. Thus, the first decimal should be correct and the second decimal should be within one unit. This is the degree of approximation one can expect for 4,000 tosses of the needle. Such a result, repeated several times, would suffice to confirm the validity of the principles involved and to indicate a mistake in a method which would lead to a result appreciably different from $1/\pi$.

A rather ingenious argument, due to Barbier, enables one to calculate without difficulty the mathematical expectation of a player who receives 1 dollar for each point at which the needle crosses one of the parallel lines. When $l < a$, he cannot get more than one such point and in this case the mathematical expectation is identical with the probability.

Let us consider an idealized object consisting of a broken line (open or closed) which is thrown at random on the parallel lines. It is clear that the mathematical expectation of a player who receives 1 dollar for each point of intersection is equal to the sum of the mathematical expectations for the individual sides of the polygon, which in turn equal the sum of the analogous expectations for the equal segments into which one can divide the sides (supposedly commensurable by the usual classical reasoning). It follows that *the desired mathematical expectation is proportional to the length of the broken line.* Now, if this reduces to a circle of diameter $2a$, the expectation equals 2, since there are always 2 and only 2 points of intersection. The length of this circle is $2\pi a$ and the mathematical expectation *per unit length* is $2/2\pi a = 1/\pi a$; for a needle of length $2l$ it is $2l/\pi a$.

To illustrate by means of an example the difference between the mathematical expectation and the probability, let us find the probability that the needle will cross at least one of the parallel lines in the case where $2l$ exceeds $2a$. Returning to Figure 11, we note that if the needle crosses at least one of the parallel lines, it must surely cross the one closest to its middle. Thus, one can assume that M lies between E and I and, using the same reasoning as above, one finds that the probability is given by the following expression

$$\frac{2}{a\pi} \int_0^a \arccos \frac{x}{l}\, dx$$

If one lets $x = l \cdot \cos t$, so that $dx = -l \cdot \sin t\, dt$, and if one lets $a = l \cdot \cos \alpha$, the value of the integral becomes

$$\frac{2l}{a\pi} \int_\alpha^{\pi/2} t \cdot \sin t\, dt = \frac{2l}{a\pi}(\sin t - t \cdot \cos t)_\alpha^{\pi/2} = \frac{2l}{a\pi}(1 - \sin \alpha + \alpha \cdot \cos \alpha)$$

It can be verified in general that this probability is less than 1; we shall verify it only for the case where l is very large compared to a, calculating for this case the asymptotic value. Having put $\cos \alpha = a/l$, one finds that

$$\sin \alpha = \left(1 - \frac{a^2}{l^2}\right)^{1/2} = 1 - \frac{a^2}{2l^2} + \dots$$

Since $\pi/2 - \alpha$ is very small and equal to $\sin\left(\dfrac{\pi}{2} - \alpha\right)$ or $\cos \alpha$ up to third-order terms, one has

$$\alpha = \frac{\pi}{2} - \frac{a}{l} + \dots$$

and the expression for the probability becomes

$$\frac{2l}{a\pi}\left[1 - \left(1 - \frac{a^2}{2l^2} + \dots\right) + \frac{a}{l}\left(\frac{\pi}{2} - \frac{a}{l} + \dots\right)\right]$$

namely,

$$\frac{2l}{a\pi}\left[\frac{a\pi}{2l} - \frac{a^2}{2l^2} + \dots\right] = 1 - \frac{a}{l\pi} + \dots$$

Also, if l is very large compared to a, the probability that there will be no intersection equals $a/\pi l$.

This result can also be established directly by observing that when l is large compared to a, the probability that the needle will cut one of the parallel lines is essentially independent of the position P of one of its extremities. Assuming P fixed, the other extremity Q must lie on the circumference of length $4\pi l$ of a circle whose center is at P and whose radius is $2l$. In order for the needle *not* to cut one of the parallel lines, Q must lie on either of the arcs RS or $R'S'$, which are contained between the same two parallel lines as the point P (see Figure 12). Now, if the radius of the circle is large compared to the distance between the parallel lines, the length of each of these arcs differs but little from the distance $2a$ between the parallel lines. The sum of their lengths is thus close to $4a$, and the probability that Q (which must lie on the circumference of length $4\pi l$) falls on one of the arcs is $4a/4\pi l = a/\pi l$. Our reasoning proves that this value is approached from below, since the true lengths of the arcs are certainly greater than $2a$.

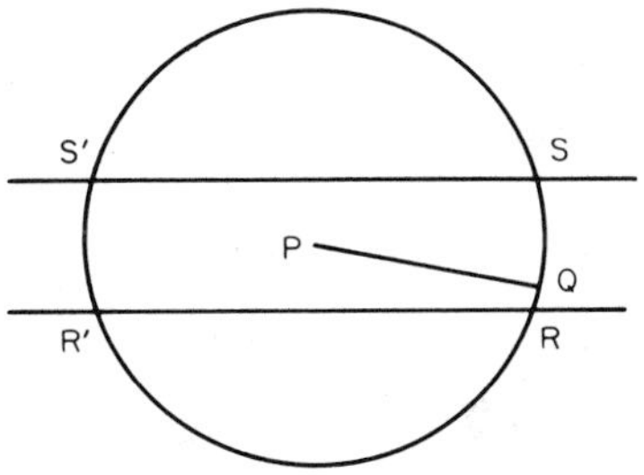

PROBLEM 30. *If a chord of a circle is selected at random, what is the probability that its length exceeds that of the side of the inscribed equilateral triangle?*

FIGURE 12

First solution. For reasons of symmetry one can arbitrarily fix the direction of the chord; thus, the point of intersection of the chord and the diameter perpendicular to its direction would have to fall on a segment equal in length to half the diameter (since the distance from the center to the side of the inscribed equilaterial triangle equals half the radius). It follows that the probability is $1/2$.

Second solution. For reasons of symmetry one can fix one of the endpoints of the chord on the circumference of the circle; thus the tangent at this point and the two sides of the inscribed equilateral triangle having this point as one of its vertices form three 60-degree angles. It follows that the chord must lie in the interior one of the three angles and, hence, that the probability is $1/3$.

Third solution. In order to determine the position of a chord it is sufficient to give its midpoint. To satisfy the given conditions it is, thus, necessary that the midpoint of the chord falls inside a circle concentric to the given circle and having half its radius. The area of this circle is $1/4$ that of the given circle and the probability is $1/4$.

Does all this mean that the three solutions are equally good or, what amounts to the same, equally bad? No, the question simply resolves to that of how an experimental verification is to be made. In other words, how does one randomly select a chord of a circle? If one tosses the chord so that it must pass through a fixed point or so that its midpoint is fixed, the second and third solutions are respectively correct. On the other hand, it is easy to see that most natural procedures one might visualize will lead to the first.

For example, if a circular disk is tossed on a plane ruled with parallel lines, the probability that one of the intersecting chords exceeds the side of the inscribed equilateral triangle is 1/2. The same result would be obtained if one looked upon the chord as the intersection of the moon and the trajectory of a star, or if one considered the chords described in the circular field of a telescope by stars to which one has not aimed and which, thus, occupy an arbitrary position. All this will be clarified further by studying the following problem, a generalization of which will be treated later on.

PROBLEM 31. *What is the probability that the length of a chord of a circle with radius R is contained between a and b?*

Given the direction of the diameter perpendicular to the chord, it can be seen that the distance from the center must be contained between $\sqrt{R^2 - \dfrac{a^2}{4}}$ and $\sqrt{R^2 - \dfrac{b^2}{4}}$. Assuming that $a < b$, the desired probability is thus

$$\frac{1}{R}\left[\sqrt{R^2 - \frac{a^2}{4}} - \sqrt{R^2 - \frac{b^2}{4}}\right]$$

The probability that the length is contained between a and $a + da$ is thus

$$-\frac{1}{R}d\left(\sqrt{R^2 - \frac{a^2}{4}}\right) = \frac{a\,da}{2R\sqrt{4R^2 - a^2}}$$

and the expected length of a chord of a circle with radius R is thus

$$\int_0^{2R} \frac{a^2\,da}{2R\sqrt{4R^2 - a^2}}$$

To evaluate this integral we substitute $a = 2R \cdot \cos \varphi$ and get

$$\int_0^{\pi/2} 2R \cdot \cos^2 \varphi\,d\varphi = \int_0^{\pi/2} R(1 + \cos 2\varphi)\,d\varphi = \frac{R\pi}{2}$$

The expected length of a chord thus equals one-fourth the circumference of the circle.

The preceding result can also be used to solve the needle problem. We shall preserve the notation of Problem 29 and limit ourselves to the case where $a = l$. AB and CD are two adjacent parallel lines (see Figure 13), EF is a perpendicular common to AB and CD, and I is the midpoint of EF. Limiting ourselves to the case where the midpoint M of the needle lies on the segment EI, we want to determine the probability that under these conditions the needle will cross AB. Drawing a circle with the center at M and having the radius $MQ = l$, we let R and S be the points of intersection of this circle and AB. Then, the desired probability equals the ratio of the arc RS to half the circumference of the circle; designating by $2c$ the length of the chord RS, we find that this ratio is given by

$$\frac{2}{\pi} \text{ arc sin } \frac{c}{l}$$

If we now designate by $\varphi(c)\, dc$ the probability that the length of a chord (of a circle of radius l) is contained between $2c$ and $2c + 2\, dc$, the total desired probability becomes

$$\int_0^l \frac{2}{\pi} \text{ arc sin } \frac{c}{l}\, \varphi(c)\, dc$$

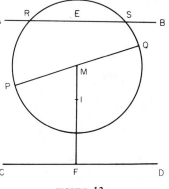

According to the preceding result (substituting $a = 2c$ and $R = l$) we now have

$$\varphi(c)\, dc = \frac{4c\, dc}{2l\sqrt{4l^2 - 4c^2}} = \frac{c\, dc}{l\sqrt{l^2 - c^2}}$$

and, upon letting $c = l \cdot \sin \theta$ the integral becomes

$$\int_0^{\pi/2} \frac{2}{\pi} \sin \theta\, d\theta = \frac{2}{\pi}$$

FIGURE 13

This agrees with the result previously obtained. If one considered the second or third solution proposed for Problem 30, one would obtain a different value for $\varphi(c)$ and, consequently, a different solution for the needle problem. Since the experimental verification is easy for these cases, this brings out the essential arbitrariness of the solutions; they correspond to very special assumptions which are seldom met in actual practice.

CHAPTER NINE

The Introduction of Arbitrary Functions

9.1 *Some General Equations*

If one makes no assumptions about experimental verifications and takes a completely abstract point of view, one can (like Poincaré) introduce an arbitrary function into the definition of probability.

Let us suppose first that we are concerned with the position of a point on a line, where the position is given by the abscissa x. If we designate by $\varphi(x)\,dx$ the probability that the abscissa is contained between x and $x + dx$, we find that the only conditions imposed a priori on the function $\varphi(x)$ are that $\varphi(x)$ must be *nonnegative* and that

$$\int_{-\infty}^{+\infty} \varphi(x)\,dx = 1$$

since x must assume some value between $-\infty$ and $+\infty$. If one knows that x must fall between a and b, one can replace this last condition by

$$\int_{a}^{b} \varphi(x)\,dx = 1$$

although this is really only a special case obtained by letting $\varphi(x)$ equal 0 from $-\infty$ to a and from b to $+\infty$.

By introducing an arbitrary function $\varphi(x)$ one overcomes all the difficulties relating to a change of variable; at least, since an analytical artifact cannot overcome real difficulties, one postpones examining these difficulties until one actually faces a concrete application. This will not cause any embarrassment, since in each problem $\varphi(x)$ will be replaced by a function determined by the conditions of the problem.

The probability that x will be contained between c and d is given by the quotient

$$\frac{\displaystyle\int_c^d \varphi(x)\,dx}{\displaystyle\int_{-\infty}^{+\infty} \varphi(x)\,dx} = \int_c^d \varphi(x)\,dx$$

where the first expression is often more convenient since $\varphi(x)$ can be replaced, without error, by a proportional quantity. Similarly, if the position of a point depends on two variables, one can introduce an arbitrary function $\varphi(x, y)$ subject to the conditions that the function must be nonnegative, that it must satisfy the relation

$$\int_{-\infty}^{+\infty} \int_{-\infty}^{+\infty} \varphi(x, y)\,dx\,dy = 1$$

and that the probability of a point (x, y) being contained in some region S is given by the double integral

$$\iint_S \varphi(x, y)\,dx\,dy$$

If x and y are replaced by polar coordinates by means of the formulas $x = r \cdot \cos \theta$ and $y = r \cdot \sin \theta$, one has only to replace $dx\,dy$ in the double integral by $r \cdot dr\,d\theta$, since

$$\frac{D(x, y)}{D(r, \theta)} = \begin{vmatrix} \dfrac{\partial x}{\partial r} & \dfrac{\partial x}{\partial \theta} \\ \dfrac{\partial y}{\partial r} & \dfrac{\partial y}{\partial \theta} \end{vmatrix} = r$$

It follows that the function $\varphi(x, y)$ must be replaced by

$$\Phi(r, \theta) = r \cdot \varphi(r \cdot \cos \theta, r \cdot \sin \theta)$$

More generally, if one lets $x = f(\alpha, \beta)$ and $y = g(\alpha, \beta)$, one obtains

$$\Phi(\alpha, \beta) = \varphi(f, g)\,\frac{D(f, g)}{D(\alpha, \beta)}$$

and the probability is now given by

$$\iint_\Sigma \Phi(\alpha, \beta)\,d\alpha\,d\beta$$

where Σ represents the region in the $\alpha\beta$-plane which corresponds to S in the xy-plane.

Imposing on φ certain conditions of continuity which we shall not discuss, one can determine a change of variable (in infinitely many ways) such that

$$\Phi(\alpha, \beta) = 1$$

Thus the probability becomes

$$\iint_\Sigma d\alpha \, d\beta$$

which makes it proportional to the area of Σ. The variables α and β thus determined are referred to as normal variables for the function $\varphi(x, y)$. Thus, for any arbitrary function there exist appropriate variables which make the function identically equal to 1, and this justifies their seemingly arbitrary choice. One must not lose sight, however, of the fact that the arbitrariness in the choice of the variables does not have a more concrete basis than the choice of the function $\varphi(x, y)$. For a given problem there are always well-determined variables which depend only on the manner in which the problem is posed.

9.2 A Case Where the Results Are Independent of the Choice of the Arbitrary Function

No matter what analytic interest there may be in the preceding considerations, this would not justify the systematic study of the introduction of arbitrary functions unless it often led to the following remarkable situation, pointed out first by Poincaré: *in certain instances the final result is largely independent of the choice of the arbitrary function.* It is necessary only that the function satisfy certain conditions concerning its continuity or variation. We shall account for this important fact by means of several examples.

PROBLEM 32. *A circular disk is divided into 2n equal sectors painted alternately black and white, and a pointer suspended at the middle of the disk is spun with sufficient speed so that it makes several complete turns before coming to rest. What is the probability that it will come to rest on one of the white sectors of the disk?*

Note that the formulation of the problem does not mention the initial position of the pointer. In fact, the result is largely independent of this position by virtue of the assumption concerning the speed with which the pointer is spun. The situation would be different if it were spun so feebly that it would cover only two or three sectors.

Let us designate by θ the total angle traversed by the pointer. Each complete turn adds 2π to this angle and, according to our assumptions, θ must always exceed several multiples of 2π. Let us now suppose that the pointer is always spun by the same person and let us designate by $\varphi(\theta) \, d\theta$ the probability that the total angle through which the pointer turns is contained between θ and $\theta + d\theta$. The function $\varphi(\theta)$ is zero for θ less than 2π, since the pointer must always make at least one complete turn. It will also be assumed that it equals zero when θ exceeds 100π or, in other words, that the person spinning the pointer with all his might cannot give it more than 50 complete turns. For values of θ between 2π and 100π we shall assume only that $\varphi(\theta)$ is *continuous*; this assumption is natural if the whole apparatus is well constructed so far as the friction acting on the pointer is concerned. If, owing to a defect in the mechanism, a greater friction acts on the pointer

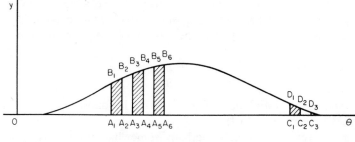

FIGURE 14

in the neighborhood of a certain value of θ, the pointer may well come to rest more frequently in that region, and if the region corresponds to a white sector of the disk, the probability that the pointer comes to rest on that sector will be affected.

We are thus making the following assumptions concerning θ: the function $y = \varphi(\theta)$ may be represented by means of a continuous curve such as the one shown in Figure 14, and

$$\int_{-\infty}^{+\infty} \varphi(\theta)\, d\theta = 1$$

We have drawn the curve of Figure 14 with a single maximum, but the reasoning which follows would be identical if it had several, though a finite, number of maxima.

Let us now consider the ordinates which correspond to the endpoints of the various subdivisions, and let us limit ourselves to the ordinates A_1B_1, $A_2B_2, \ldots$, and A_6B_6. By assumption, the interval contained between A_1B_1 and A_2B_2 corresponds to a black sector and it is shaded in Figure 14; the interval contained between A_2B_2 and A_3B_3 corresponds to a white sector, and so forth.

Denoting by p the probability that the pointer comes to rest on a white sector and by q the probability that it comes to rest on a black sector, we find that

$$\frac{p}{q} = \frac{\sum \text{area } A_2B_2A_3B_3}{\sum \text{area } A_1B_1A_2B_2}$$

where the sum in the numerator extends over all the areas that are not shaded, while the sum in the denominator extends over all the areas that are shaded.

It is easy to show that the ratio p/q is very close to 1, and that it approaches 1 when n grows large. This can be done in several ways. First, let us base our argument on the continuity of the function $\varphi(\theta)$. When n is large and the function is continuous, the ratio of two adjacent areas is very close to 1 since $\varphi(\theta)$ varies but very little when θ varies by $2\pi/n$. It is true that at the ends where the curve approaches the axis a small absolute difference can yield a ratio differing appreciably from 1 (see areas $C_1D_1C_2D_2$ and $C_2D_2C_3D_3$ in Figure 14), but these small areas can be ignored without introducing an appreciable error. The ratio p/q can thus be written

$$\frac{p}{q} = \frac{\sum p_n}{\sum q_n}$$

where each of the ratios p_n/q_n is close to 1. It follows that the ratio p/q itself must be very close to 1.

A way of reasoning that is perhaps somewhat more satisfactory (and more rigorous) makes use of the variation of the function $\varphi(\theta)$. Referring to our figure, it can be seen that

$$\text{area } A_1B_1A_2B_2 < \text{area } A_2B_2A_3B_3 < \text{area } A_3B_3A_4B_4 < \ldots$$

Thus, if one designates the area corresponding to the white sectors by $p_1, p_2, \ldots, p_n, \ldots$, and the areas corresponding to the black sectors by $q_1, q_2, \ldots, q_n, \ldots$, one finds that

$$p_1 < q_1 < p_2 < q_2 < \ldots < p_n < q_n < \ldots$$

assuming that the first area on the left is white. These inequalities continue until one reaches the maximum of the curve, after which they are reversed. It follows that

$$\frac{p_1}{q_1} < 1, \qquad \frac{p_2}{q_2} < 1, \qquad \frac{p_3}{q_3} < 1, \qquad \ldots, \qquad \frac{p_n}{q_n} < 1$$

and, hence, that

$$\rho_n = \frac{p_1 + p_2 + \ldots + p_n}{q_1 + q_2 + \ldots + q_n} < 1$$

On the other hand, one has

$$\frac{p_2}{q_1} > 1, \qquad \frac{p_3}{q_2} > 1, \qquad \ldots, \qquad \frac{p_{n+1}}{q_n} > 1$$

and, hence,

$$\rho_n' = \frac{p_2 + p_3 + \ldots + p_{n+1}}{q_1 + q_2 + \ldots + q_n} > 1$$

Calculating the difference between the ratios ρ'_n and ρ_n one obtains

$$\rho'_n - \rho_n = \frac{p_{n+1} - p_1}{q_1 + q_2 + \ldots + q_n}$$

and this quantity becomes smaller and smaller when n becomes large. Designating this difference by ϵ_n, we now have

$$\rho_n < 1 < \rho'_n \qquad \text{and} \qquad \rho'_n - \rho_n = \epsilon_n$$

It follows that each of the differences $\rho'_n - 1$ and $1 - \rho_n$ is less than ϵ_n. The same reasoning applies also to the decreasing portion of the curve and, hence, to the total ratio. Thus, the required probability equals 1/2; this result is approximate under the given assumptions, but it is to a large measure independent of the choice of the arbitrary function.

PROBLEM 33. *If one constructs a table of a function $\varphi(x)$ for values of x increasing by very small steps (say, for $x = 0, 0.00001, 0.00002, 0.00003$, etc.), what is the probability that the second decimal of an entry in this table is a 7?*

Note that the problem refers to an arbitrary function $\varphi(x)$, which need not be given. Making use of the law of the mean one has

$$\varphi(x_2) - \varphi(x_1) = (x_2 - x_1)\varphi'(\xi)$$

where ξ denotes a number between x_1 and x_2. For example, in order that the second decimal be a 7, it is necessary that $\varphi(x)$ be contained between 1.37 and 1.38.* According to the preceding formula, the interval of variation for x is thus

$$x_2 - x_1 = \frac{0.01}{\varphi'(\xi)}$$

Assuming that x varies by intervals of 0.00001, we find that the number of values of x contained in this interval is given by the integral part of $1{,}000/\varphi'(\xi)$, where ξ is such that $\varphi(\xi)$ is contained between 1.37 and 1.38. Let us denote it ξ_{37}. The total number of values of x for which the second decimal digit is a 7 is thus given by

$$x_7 = \frac{1{,}000}{\varphi'(\xi_{17})} + \frac{1{,}000}{\varphi'(\xi_{27})} + \frac{1{,}000}{\varphi'(\xi_{37})} + \ldots$$

where the number of terms is determined by the extent of the variation of the function φ within the table. Similarly, the number of values of x for which the second decimal digit is an 8 is given by

$$x_8 = \frac{1{,}000}{\varphi'(\xi_{18})} + \frac{1{,}000}{\varphi'(\xi_{28})} + \ldots$$

---

* If one has a table where the figures are rounded to four decimals, for example, the second decimal will actually be a 7 when the true value of the function $\varphi(x)$ lies between 1.36995 and 1.37995; this makes no appreciable difference.

The ratio of the probability p_7 that the second digit is a 7 to the probability p_8 that the digit is an 8 is equal to the ratio x_7/x_8, but if one puts

$$\frac{1}{\varphi'(x)} = \Phi(x)$$

one has

$$\frac{x_7}{x_8} = \frac{\sum \Phi(\xi_{37})}{\sum \Phi(\xi_{38})}$$

Assuming that $\Phi(x)$ is continuous, reasoning analogous to that used in the preceding problem proves that this ratio is very close to 1; the probability p_7 is thus approximately $1/10$.

As an application one might determine how often a given digit occurs in the fifth decimal in a table of logarithms given to seven decimals. One would find that the probability for each digit is very close to $1/10$.

9.3 *Application to the Distribution of the Minor Planets*

If one wants to investigate how the minor planets are distributed over the zodiac, the problem may be simplified by restating it as follows:

PROBLEM 34. *If one considers n points moving uniformly (but with different speeds) along the circumference of a circle, what is the mathematical expectation of a person who is to receive as many dollars as there are points on a given arc?*

Note that in a given instance the probability that any one point is on the arc is proportional to the length α of the arc and, since its motion is uniform, the time a point spends on the arc is proportional to its length. The mathematical expectation is thus $\alpha/2\pi$ for each point and $n\alpha/2\pi$ for all n points. One could be satisfied with this solution, which I have also discussed in one of my other books, but let us examine how Poincaré approaches this subject: he looks for the mean of a periodic function of the curvilinear abscissa α of one of the points—say, for example, $\sin \alpha$. It is clear that the corresponding mean for n points approaches zero when their distribution becomes more and more uniform. Now, if one denotes by a_k the abscissa of one at the points at the time $t = 0$ and by b_k its angular velocity, its curvilinear abscissa is $a_k + b_k t$ and the desired mean value becomes

$$\frac{1}{n} \sum \sin (a_k + b_k t)$$

Assuming that the number of points is very large, the method of Poincaré consists of replacing this sum by an integral; designating by $\varphi(x, y) \, dx \, dy$ the number of points for which a_k is contained between x and $x + dx$ and

b_k is contained between y and $y + dy$, one can write

$$\sum \sin (a_k + b_k t) = \iint \sin (x + ty) \varphi(x, y) \, dx \, dy$$

$$n = \iint \varphi(x, y) \, dx \, dy$$

where both of these double integrals extend over the entire domain for which $\varphi(x, y)$ is not equal to zero. The desired mean value is thus given by

$$\frac{\iint \sin (x + ty) \varphi(x, y) \, dx \, dy}{\iint \varphi(x, y) \, dx \, dy}$$

and it can easily be shown that when t increases indefinitely the mean value tends to zero. Thus, even if the distribution is not uniform at the start, it tends to become uniform.

This argument has been given in spite of certain objections which I have discussed elsewhere. These objections are analogous to those which arise in the study of the kinetic theory of gases, and I shall not discuss them here.

9.4 Application to the Kinetic Theory of Gases

The study of the motion of n molecules in three-dimensional space may be looked upon as the study of the motion of one point in $3n$-dimensional space. The most important features of this problem may be brought out by studying the motion of a point in a space of only two dimensions, that is, in the plane, and we shall limit ourselves to this case.

Suppose that a point mass is moving rectilinearly in the plane and that x and y are its rectangular coordinates. We shall look for the probability that the integral parts of x and y are even integers; that is, the probability that x and y are contained between 0 and 1, between 2 and 3, between 4 and 5, and so on.

If we divide the first quadrant into a network of squares of side 1, we can shade the squares for which the preceding condition is satisfied and state simply that we are looking for the probability that the moving point is inside one of the shaded squares (see Figure 15).

It is worth noting that if one considers a point mass restricted to uniform rectilinear motion inside a square and reflected in accordance with the classical laws of mechanics, its movement is entirely analogous to that of the point mass we have considered. To indicate the ·identity of the two problems one has only to suppose that one observes the motion of a point inside the square by means of mirrors erected perpendicularly on its edges. Note also that the problem would be the same if we consider a point mass inside a cube which is reflected in accordance with the classical laws, and focus our attention on the projection of the point on a face of the cube. In what follows, we shall limit ourselves to studying the problem as it was formulated first.

If α and β are the coordinates of the point at $t = 0$ and u and v are the projections of its velocity on the coordinate axes, its coordinates at time t are given by the formulas

$$x = \alpha + ut, \qquad y = \beta + vt$$

Although it is quite interesting in certain respects, we shall not discuss the case where α, β, u, and v are known without error. Some arithmetical properties of these numbers—for example, the question whether they are commensurable or not—would enter this discussion. Of course, this would not be a practical problem, since the assumption that a number is known with absolute precision is a purely theoretical concept without any real significance. In actual practice, one must regard α, β, u, and v as known only to a certain degree of approximation, although for the sake of brevity we shall assume that α and β are known without error;

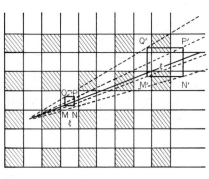

FIGURE 15

this will have no appreciable effect on the results. Thus, we shall designate by ϵ and η the maximum absolute errors for u and v and write the preceding formulas as

$$x = \alpha + u't, \qquad |u' - u| \leqslant \epsilon$$
$$y = \beta + v't, \qquad |v' - v| \leqslant \eta$$

If ω is the point whose coordinates are α and β, ξ is the point whose coordinates are $\alpha + u'$ and $\beta + v'$, and u' and v' assume all possible values (that is, u' varies from $u - \epsilon$ to $u + \epsilon$ and v' from $v - \eta$ to $v + \eta$), the point ξ fills the interior of a rectangle $MNPQ$, whose sides are of length 2ϵ and 2η, respectively. By assumption, the point ξ can occupy any position inside this rectangle, and we shall assume that the probability that it is in a certain region is proportional to the area of that region. Using the argument of Poincaré (see Section 7.3), it can be seen that this assumption is not essential, but it nevertheless simplifies the reasoning as well as the calculations.

It is easy to see where the point ξ', whose coordinates are $x = \alpha + u't$ and $y = \beta + v't$, is located. This point is homothetic to ξ, with the center of projectivity being the point ω and the ratio of homotheticity being equal to t; it is the interior of the rectangle $M'N'P'Q'$, which is homothetic to the rectangle $MNPQ$ in the same ratio. We had to draw Figure 15 so that t is only a few units, but it is easy to visualize what happens when t equals thousands or millions of units. No matter how small $MNPQ$ might be, the rectangle $M'N'P'Q'$, whose dimensions are t times larger, becomes very large compared to the squares of the network, and the shaded squares occupy nearly one-fourth of its area. The validity of this argument increases with t, since the areas of the squares partially inside and partially outside become negligible compared to the total area of the squares that fall inside.

This demonstrates how time brings about an equalization of probabilities, so long as there is an initial indeterminance, no matter how small. For small values of t—for example, for the rectangle $M'N'P'Q'$ of Figure 15—one might obtain a shaded portion less than 1/4. This does not equal the theoretical value, but there is a tendency among the probabilities to equalize when t assumes greater and greater values. It is by means of an analogous mechanism that molecules, as one considers them in the kinetic theory, tend to arrange themselves in a distribution which calculations show to be most probable. One cannot actually demonstrate that such a most probable distribution is realized at a given moment, but if it is not realized one can say that the practical probability of the existing distribution is zero. One can demonstrate, however, that regardless of what distribution there may exist at a given moment, the probability that the most probable distribution will be realized at a later time is so close to 1 that it can be put equal to 1. The same reasoning applies also to prior moments, though with the following difference: When one calculates a future state from a present state, the present state is not rigorously known, and the small limits of error within which the present state is known make it possible to calculate various probabilities concerning the future state. After all, one cannot really speak of probabilities unless something is unknown. On the other hand, if one wants to reconstruct a prior state from a present state, the uncertainty is greater; in the preceding case where we knew the prior state, we learned more about the present state than we would have by a direct study of that state. For example, if one has two containers, one empty and one full, and if one allows their contents to mix by opening a stop, the resulting state will not permit any conclusions about a state prior to the opening of the stop. It is known with a precision exceeding experimental possibilities that the most minute modification in the present state could well lead to an entirely different prior state. Thus, it is impossible to define and calculate the probability of a prior state by a method analogous to the one used above.

CHAPTER TEN

Errors of Measurement

10.1 *Formulation of the Problem*

We shall not go into all questions arising in a complete theory of errors of measurement, since this would require a book in itself. In particular we shall not give any of the details concerning the mathematical calculations required to deduce from a number of measurements the value of the quantity they are supposed to estimate. Neither shall we go into the theoretical discussions surrounding the law of Laplace-Gauss or the mathematical developments to which these discussions have led.* The importance of the results thus obtained is not proportional to the analytical effort required, and this is one of the main reasons for the practical pseudouniversality often attached to the law of Laplace-Gauss.†

Having pointed out this reason, we shall limit ourselves to the development of the most important theoretical consequences of the law of Laplace-Gauss. Among the three parts which constitute the complete theory, namely, the derivation of the law, its theoretical investigation, and its applications, we shall limit ourselves mainly to the second.

---

* For a long time this law has been referred to as the law of Gauss. Although the law was first formulated by Laplace, Gauss' research in this area has become classic.

† The following is the main reason why it is best not to go into these questions of complicated analytical reasoning (the integration of differential equations, functional equations, etc.) except with great prudence. Approximations can provide valid reasoning under some conditions, but these conditions are not always met. Whereas one can readily control errors in equations which follow algebraically from equations which themselves permit errors, the same cannot be said for differential equations or functional equations. Here a slight modification in one equation can change the entire analytic nature of the integral.

10.2 *The Law of Laplace-Gauss*

Suppose one wants to measure a quantity, say, a length, whose true value is a; if the measurement equals a' the error is $a' - a$, and according to the law of Laplace-Gauss the probability that this error is contained between x and $x + dx$ is given by

$$\frac{k}{\sqrt{\pi}} e^{-k^2 x^2} dx$$

where k is a constant called the *precision* of the method of measurement being used.

This formulation of the law calls for several observations. First of all, what does one mean by the *true* value of the quantity that is being measured? Since this value is usually unknown before any measurements are made, is it not a vicious circle to evaluate the errors of measurement with the aid of a number furnished by the measurements themselves? We shall not dwell on this problem, which can be tied in with the probability of causes; let us merely indicate that there are situations where this difficulty does not exist. For the moment, at least, we shall limit ourselves to such cases, namely, to cases where the quantity to be measured might be known from prior measurements (or from theoretical considerations) to a greater degree of precision than that provided by the measurements themselves. A situation like this might arise in physics or chemistry where numerous students are asked to determine a physical constant well known in advance.

The same can be said for the constant k appearing in the formula of Laplace. It is generally known only after some observations have been made, and we shall indicate later how it might be estimated.

The law of Laplace gives the same probability to positive and negative errors, that is, to errors whose absolute values are the same. It is only when this symmetry is realized that one can assume that the law applies.

Finally, let us observe that if x is replaced by a function of x the analytical form of the law can be modified. This objection is analogous to the ones we have already met and it must be answered in the same way: by the observation of facts. For instance, if one uses a ruler to measure a length, the various parts of the ruler are homogeneous, and it is not the square of the length that is being measured, but the length itself. Thus, it is relative to the length, and not to the square of the length, that the error pertains.

Nevertheless, when the errors are small the formula of Laplace preserves its form to a *first-order approximation*. If we let

$$b = \varphi(a), \qquad b' = \varphi(a')$$
$$x = a' - a, \qquad y = b' - b$$

we have

$$y = \varphi'(\alpha)x$$

where α is a number contained between a and a'. If all the values a' are contained in an interval that is sufficiently small, one has for all practical purposes $\varphi'(\alpha) = \varphi'(a) = c$, and the law becomes

$$\frac{k}{\sqrt{\pi}} e^{-k^2 x^2} \, dx = \frac{k}{c\sqrt{\pi}} e^{-k^2 y^2 / c^2} \, dy$$

It follows that the precision is simply divided by c. Suppose, for example, that one measures a length of 100 feet and that the measurements differ among themselves by at most 1 foot. If one refers to the square of the length rather than to the length itself, one has $\varphi(a) = a^2$, $\varphi'(a) = 2a$, and it can be seen that the value of c is contained between 199 and 201. Thus, one commits a relative error in the neighborhood of $1/200$ if one puts c equal to 200.

10.3 *Foundation of the Law of Laplace*

One could be satisfied by saying that in certain instances the law of Laplace is justified by experience, in which case one might refer to a series of measurements as *normal* if they follow the law of Laplace, and as *nonnormal* if they do not. Having made this definition, one is perfectly justified in basing a theory for series of normal measurements on the law of Laplace. Some persons may feel that by doing this one is simply making use of one's right to give definitions for one's own use. Others may feel that this simply replaces the difficulty, which cannot be resolved by means of a linguistic convention no matter how ingenious, with another one, and that the real point in question is how to know why it happens so often that series of measurements are actually normal. This is what we shall briefly explain, setting aside another, more difficult, question to which we shall return in Part III, namely, that of investigating the intrinsic character of a normal series of measurements. Indeed, only after we shall have found in a normal series of measurements a characteristic other than its following the law of Laplace, will this question become instructive and its importance exceed that of an abstract linguistic convention.

The fact that certain series of measurements are normal follows from the results we have obtained in Part I, where we demonstrated that if one makes n_1 drawings from an urn with the probability p_1, n_2 drawings from an urn with the probability p_2, etc., the relative deviation λ will follow a normal law (the law of Laplace with $k = 1$), and that the absolute deviation λU equals the product of the relative deviation and the unit deviation U defined by the relation

$$U^2 = 2n_1 p_1 q_1 + 2n_2 p_2 q_2 + \cdots$$

Now, what happens when one performs a measurement? The causes for errors are very numerous, each of them has a certain probability, and each can produce an error of a certain size. If one cause can produce errors having two different values, one can regard the two errors as resulting, so to speak, from the two distinct causes having distinct probabilities. If the error produced by a cause varies continuously, one can decompose its domain of variation into a number of elements which are sufficiently small so that within each element the error may be regarded as constant. Then one designates by n_1 the number of possible errors whose value is α_1 and whose probability is p_1, by n_2 the number of possible errors whose value is α_2 and whose probability is p_2, and so on. The numbers α_1, α_2, . . . can be either positive or negative, and one has

$$n_1 p_1 \alpha_1 + n_2 p_2 \alpha_2 + \ldots = 0$$

so that the total error is zero if each partial error occurs in accordance with its probability. This is a consequence of the hypothesis, indispensable if the law of Laplace is to hold, that the negative errors are as probable as the positive errors.

In reality, the errors α_1 do not occur $n_1 p_1$ times, but $n_1 p_1 + \lambda_1 u_1$ times, where $u_1 = \sqrt{2 n_1 p_1 q_1}$ is the partial unit deviation and the relative deviation λ_1 satisfies the law of Laplace (see Section 5.1), and so forth. One concludes that the error is

$$\lambda U = \lambda_1 u_1 \alpha_1 + \lambda_2 u_2 \alpha_2 + \ldots + \lambda_k u_k \alpha_k$$

and reasoning analogous to that of Sections 5.6 and 5.7 yields

$$U^2 = u_1^2 \alpha_1^2 + u_2^2 \alpha_2^2 + \ldots + u_k^2 \alpha_k^2$$

The quantity U thus defined is the unit deviation and the relative deviation follows the law of Laplace. It can be seen that the unit deviation U is the reciprocal of the quantity k which we referred to as the precision. This follows from the fact that the probability for λ is

$$\frac{1}{\sqrt{\pi}} e^{-\lambda^2} \, d\lambda$$

and, hence, that the probability for $x = \lambda U$ is

$$\frac{1}{U \sqrt{\pi}} e^{-x^2/U^2} \, dx$$

Thus, one has

$$\frac{1}{k^2} = \sum 2 n_i p_i q_i \alpha_i^2$$

so that, roughly speaking, the precision is inversely proportional to the values of the elementary errors and to the square root of their number. If the elementary errors are all divided by 10, the precision is multiplied by 10; if the elementary errors remain of the same size but become 100 times more numerous, the precision is divided by 10. These remarks will become more meaningful after we have studied the relationship between reality and the number k which we called the precision, and which until now has been nothing but the definition of an abstract term (see also Section 10.5).

To summarize, the law of Laplace is justified by the fact that when the possible errors are numerous, their combinations are subject to the law which we obtained by combinatorial analysis in the case where we studied a great number of repeated trials.

10.4 *Invariance of the Law of Laplace*

An *a posteriori* justification of the law of Laplace may be found in the following invariance property: *when the errors of measurement of several quantities individually follow the law of Laplace, the same is true also for the error of their sum.* It will suffice to prove this for two quantities, for which the probabilities of obtaining an error between x and $x + dx$ and y and $y + dy$ are, respectively,

$$\frac{k}{\sqrt{\pi}}\, e^{-k^2 x^2}\, dx \qquad \text{and} \qquad \frac{k'}{\sqrt{\pi}}\, e^{-k'^2 y^2}\, dy$$

What is the probability that the error for the sum of the two quantities is contained between z and $z + dz$? If the error for the first quantity is equal to x, the error for the second must be contained between $z - x$ and $z - x + dz$, and the corresponding probability is

$$\frac{k'}{\sqrt{\pi}}\, e^{-k'^2(z-x)^2}\, dz$$

Now, the total probability is obtained by multiplying this expression by the probability that the first error is contained between x and $x + dx$, and then integrating on x from $-\infty$ to $+\infty$. This will give an expression of the form $J\, dz$, where

$$J = \frac{kk'}{\pi} \int_{-\infty}^{+\infty} e^{-k'^2(z-x)^2 - k^2 x^2}\, dx$$

and, using the results obtained in Section 5.6, this may be written as

$$J = \frac{k''}{\sqrt{\pi}}\, e^{-k''^2 z^2}$$

where the precision k'' is given by

$$\frac{1}{k''^2} = \frac{1}{k^2} + \frac{1}{k'^2}$$

10.5 *The Precision of a Series of Measurements*

Let us now demonstrate the significance of the coefficient k which we have referred to as the *precision*. The probability that an error is contained between $k\lambda_1$ and $k\lambda_2$ is

$$\frac{k}{\sqrt{\pi}} \int_{k\lambda_1}^{k\lambda_2} e^{-k^2 x^2}\, dx = \frac{1}{\sqrt{\pi}} \int_{\lambda_1}^{\lambda_2} e^{-\lambda^2}\, d\lambda$$

which is independent of k. Thus, when the precision of a system of measurements is 10 times that of another system, this means that the probability that an error of the first system is contained between certain limits equals the probability that an error of the second system is contained between limits 10 times as wide. For example, errors of a certain number of millimeters in the first system would have the same probability as corresponding errors in centimeters in the second system.

The *probable error* (or *expected error*) is by definition the sum of the products obtained by multiplying each possible value by the corresponding probability. If one allows for the signs of the errors, the probable error is zero since the positive errors are as probable as the negative errors. If one takes their absolute values, the probable error is

$$\frac{2k}{\sqrt{\pi}} \int_0^\infty e^{-k^2 z^2}\, dz = \frac{1}{k\sqrt{\pi}}$$

As should have been expected, the probable error is small when the precision is large. Given n observations for which the absolute errors are $e_1, e_2, \ldots$, and e_n, the probable error may be approximated by their mean, that is, by writing

$$\frac{1}{k\sqrt{\pi}} = \frac{e_1 + e_2 + \cdots + e_n}{n}$$

and this also enables one to estimate the precision k.

Similarly, the probable or mean value of the square of the error is given by

$$\frac{2k}{\sqrt{\pi}} \int_0^\infty e^{-k^2 z^2}\, dz = \frac{1}{2k^2}$$

and its value is estimated (approximated) by means of the formula

$$\frac{1}{2k^2} = \frac{e_1^2 + e_2^2 + \ldots + e_n^2}{n}$$

One can improve on these approximations by determining the value of σ for which the square of the difference

$$\frac{1}{k\sqrt{\pi}} - \sigma \cdot \frac{e_1 + e_2 + \ldots + e_n}{n}$$

has the smallest probable value. In other words, one must determine σ so that it minimizes the expression

$$\mathbf{m}\left(\frac{1}{k\sqrt{\pi}} - \sigma \cdot \frac{e_1 + e_2 + \ldots + e_n}{n} \right)^2$$

Making use of the fact that

$$\mathbf{m}(1) = 1, \quad \mathbf{m}(e_i) = \frac{1}{k\sqrt{\pi}}, \quad \mathbf{m}(e_i e_j) = \frac{1}{k^2 \pi}, \quad \mathbf{m}(e_i^2) = \frac{1}{2k^2}$$

the quantity to be minimized becomes

$$\frac{1}{k^2\pi} - \frac{2\sigma}{k^2\pi} + \frac{\sigma^2}{\pi^2}\left(\frac{n}{2k^2} + \frac{n(n-1)}{k^2\pi}\right)$$

which equals

$$\frac{1}{k^2\pi}\left[1 - 2\sigma + \sigma^2\left(\frac{\pi - 2}{2n} + 1\right)\right]$$

The minimum corresponds to

$$\sigma = \frac{1}{1 + \dfrac{\pi - 2}{2n}}$$

and its value is

$$\frac{1}{2\pi k^2 n^2}\left(1 - \frac{2}{\pi}\right)\frac{1}{1 + \dfrac{\pi - 2}{2n}}$$

Thus, if one uses the formula

$$\frac{1}{k\sqrt{\pi}} = \frac{1}{1 + \dfrac{\pi - 2}{2n}} \cdot \frac{e_1 + e_2 + \ldots + e_n}{n}$$

one can expect to make the smallest error in estimating the precision. This is not of great practical significance; if n is large the two estimates are almost the same, and if n is small they are both very uncertain.

10.6 *Weights and Means*

The name *weight* is usually given to the square k^2 of the precision k, and this is justified by the solution of the following problem.

PROBLEM 37. *Two series of measurements are made to measure a given length z, and their respective precisions are k and k'. Given only one measurement m of the first series and one measurement m' of the second series, how should one combine these two values to obtain an estimate of z?*

For obvious reasons, one is led to estimate z by means of an expression of the form*

$$z = \frac{hm + h'm'}{h + h'}$$

---

* In fact, the expression for z should satisfy the following conditions: (1) if m and m' are multiplied by a constant, z should also be multiplied by that constant; in other words, the expression should be homogeneous to the first degree; (2) if a constant is added to m as well as to m', it should also be added to z; in other words, the expression should be linear as well as homogeneous; (3) if $m = m'$, z must equal their common value.

where h and h' are called the *weights* of the respective measurements. If one denotes by x and y the errors of these two measurements, the error committed by z is

$$\frac{hx + h'y}{h + h'}$$

We shall not try to minimize the probable value of this expression; its probable value is zero since the errors x and y have to be taken with their signs. Instead, we shall minimize the probable value of its square, namely,

$$\mathbf{m}\left(\frac{hx + h'y}{h + h'}\right)^2 = \frac{h^2\mathbf{m}(x^2) + h'^2\mathbf{m}(y^2)}{(h + h')^2}$$

since the mean value of xy is zero. Since

$$\mathbf{m}(x^2) = \frac{1}{2k^2} \quad\text{and}\quad \mathbf{m}(y^2) = \frac{1}{2k'^2}$$

the quantity to be minimized becomes

$$\left(\frac{h^2}{k^2} + \frac{h'^2}{k'^2}\right)\frac{1}{(h + h')^2}$$

and if one lets $h = u(h + h')$ and $h' = (1 - u)(h + h')$, the expression becomes

$$\frac{u^2}{k^2} + \frac{(1 - u)^2}{k'^2}$$

Equating to zero its derivative with respect to u, one obtains

$$\frac{u}{k^2} - \frac{1 - u}{k'^2} = 0$$

that is to say,

$$\frac{h}{k^2} = \frac{h'}{k'^2}$$

The *weights* h and h' are thus proportional to k^2 and k'^2, and the desired value of z is

$$z = \frac{k^2m + k'^2m'}{k^2 + k'^2}$$

If several observations belong to the same series and thus have the same precision, they are combined by means of the formula for the arithmetic mean.

More generally, if n_1 observations have the precision k_1 and the mean α_1, n_2 observations have the precision k_2 and the mean α_2, and so on, the corresponding value for z is given by

$$z = \frac{n_1k_1^2\alpha_1 + \ldots + n_pk_p^2\alpha_p}{n_1k_1^2 + \ldots + n_pk_p^2}$$

Thus, the weight of a set of observations is obtained by multiplying their common weight by their number. One also concludes from this that the precision of the mean of several observations equals the product of the precision of an individual observation and the square root of the number of observations. This important result may be obtained directly as follows: if

$$x = x_1 + x_2 + \ldots + x_n$$

and $k_1, k_2, \ldots, k_n$, and k are the precisions corresponding to the errors $x_1, x_2, \ldots, x_n$, and their sum x, one has

$$\frac{1}{k^2} = \frac{1}{k_1^2} + \frac{1}{k_2^2} + \ldots + \frac{1}{k_n^2}$$

Now, if one assumes that $k_1 = k_2 = \ldots = k_n$, this formula gives

$$k = \frac{k_1}{\sqrt{n}}$$

but the precision of x/n is n times as large as that of x (since an error in x corresponds to an error n times as small in x/n). Thus, the precision of the mean x/n is $nk = k_1\sqrt{n}$.

For example, the mean of 100 measurements has a precision 10 times that of an individual measurement, and the mean of 10,000 measurements has a precision 100 times that of an individual measurement. We shall not consider the problem of determining what limiting precision can be attained in *actual practice* by increasing the number of measurements.

CHAPTER ELEVEN

The Problem of Choice in the Continuum

11.1 *The Continuum*

Rapid progress in differential and integral calculus has enabled mathematicians to treat many problems with reference to a continuum rather than with reference to very large finite numbers. This has been the case, for example, in the theory of elasticity, where, instead of considering innumerable molecules, one performs calculations with differential elements $dx\,dy\,dz$ considered infinitely small, but nevertheless containing so many molecules that matter can be looked upon as homogeneous.

The same argument holds also for the theory of continuous probabilities, which can often be substituted for the theory of discrete probabilities in situations involving very large numbers, for which the calculations would otherwise be long and often prohibitive.

From the point of view of the physicist, whose measuring instruments permit an accuracy to 7 or 8 decimals, a length of a yard may be looked upon as formed by millions upon millions of equal segments; each of these segments is comparable to a geometrical point, as it is physically impossible to distinguish between individual points. Choosing a point at randon on a segment whose length is a yard is thus equivalent to choosing one of these small segments from among millions of identical segments, namely, a problem of discrete probabilities. It will be easy to see that most practical problems to which one applies the theory of continuous probabilities are similar in nature to the case we shall discuss. The difficulties we shall meet presently with reference to a choice in the continuum do not arise in these problems, and this is why we did not meet them in the preceding chapters. Nevertheless, these difficulties are of great interest with respect to the very founda-tions of scientific knowledge, and this is why we shall study them, after having given a simple example of an important case where calculations for the discrete case give in the limit important results for continuous probabilities.

11.2 *The Law of Poisson*

Let us consider a line segment AB of unit length and on it an unknown number of points P. It is known only that the probability of a point P falling on an infinitesimal segment of length dx is $\lambda\,dx$, and it is desired to calculate the probability that there are exactly k such points P on AB.

We shall treat this problem first as a problem of discrete probabilities, dividing the segment AB into n equal parts, where n is large. The proba-bility p that a point P falls on one of these segments is λ/n, and we shall assume that n is so large compared to λ that the probability p is extremely small; the probability that none of the points P falls on such a segment is $1 - p$.

Let us now choose k of the n segments, and let us suppose that there is a point P on each of these k segments but none on any of the other $n - k$ segments. The probability for such an arrangement is $p^k(1 - p)^{n-k}$, and we know that the number of ways in which the k segments can be chosen from a set of n is

$$C_n^k = \frac{n!}{k!(n-k)!}$$

The probability P_k that there are k points on exactly k of the n segments, where the k segments are arbitrary and not chosen in advance, is thus

$$P_k = \frac{n!}{k!(n-k)!}\,p^k(1-p)^{n-k} = \frac{n!}{k!(n-k)!}\left(\frac{\lambda}{n}\right)^k\left(1-\frac{\lambda}{n}\right)^{n-k}$$

Observing that

$$\frac{n!}{(n-k)!} = n(n-1)\cdot\ldots\cdot(n-k+1) = n^k\left(1-\frac{1}{n}\right)\cdot\ldots\cdot\left(1-\frac{k-1}{n}\right)$$

one can write

$$P_k = \frac{\lambda^k}{k!}\left(1-\frac{1}{n}\right)\left(1-\frac{2}{n}\right)\cdot\ldots\cdot\left(1-\frac{k-1}{n}\right)\left(1-\frac{\lambda}{n}\right)^{n-k}$$

Suppose now that n increases indefinitely while λ and k remain fixed. One thus has

$$\lim_{n\to\infty}\left(1-\frac{\lambda}{n}\right)^n = e^{-\lambda}$$

and the product

$$\left(1-\frac{1}{n}\right)\cdot\ldots\cdot\left(1-\frac{k-1}{n}\right)\left(1-\frac{\lambda}{n}\right)^{-k}$$

evidently approaches 1 as it consists of a finite number of factors, each having the limit 1. We thus get

$$P_k = \frac{\lambda^k}{k!} e^{-\lambda}$$

and this is the formula of Poisson. It should be noted that

$$P_0 + P_1 + \ldots + P_k + \ldots = e^{-\lambda}\left(1 + \frac{\lambda}{1} + \frac{\lambda^2}{2!} + \ldots + \frac{\lambda^k}{k!} + \ldots\right) = 1$$

since the quantity in parentheses equals e^λ.

Regardless of the choice of $\lambda > 0$, there can be any number of points P on the segment AB, and the sum of the probabilities equals 1, as it should. It should also be noted that when k is sufficiently large compared to λ, P_k will rapidly tend to zero, and the probability will become negligible after a certain value of k. Let us now consider the ratio

$$\frac{P_k}{P_{k+1}} = \frac{\lambda}{k+1}$$

If λ is not an integer, P_k will increase until k equals the integral part of λ; after that P_{k+1} will be less than P_k and this will continue indefinitely. If λ is an integer, the values of $P_{\lambda-1}$ and P_λ are equal and they constitute the maximum values of the function P_k.

Poisson's formula may be applied to problems of repeated trials when the number of trials is very large, the probability of a success on an individual trial is very small, and λ designates the total mathematical expectation. Without making an appreciable error, the formula of Poisson may thus be used when the number of trials is sufficiently large and the probability p is sufficiently small. An interesting special case arises when $\lambda = 1$. For example, one might buy one lot each from 100 lotteries, where each lottery issues 100 lots, or one might bet 37 times on a given number in roulette, where there are 36 numbers and zero. What is the probability of winning not even once, the probability of winning exactly once, exactly twice, and so forth? Rounding to as many decimals as shown, we have

$$P_0 = 1/e = 0.368$$
$$P_1 = P_0 = 0.368$$
$$P_2 = \tfrac{1}{2}P_1 = 0.184$$
$$P_3 = \tfrac{1}{3}P_2 = 0.061$$
$$P_4 = \tfrac{1}{4}P_3 = 0.015$$
$$P_5 = \tfrac{1}{5}P_4 = 0.003$$
$$P_6 = \tfrac{1}{6}P_5 = 0.0005$$
$$\overline{\qquad\qquad 0.9995}$$

When λ is sufficiently large and, for the sake of simplicity, assumed to be a whole number, one can easily obtain the approximate formula

$$P_\lambda = \frac{1}{\sqrt{2\pi\lambda}}$$

and it can be shown that the law of Laplace-Gauss applies to the deviations from λ.

11.3 *The Choice of a Point on a Line Segment*

As has already been pointed out, we are led to say in the theory of discrete probabilities that a point is randomly selected on a line segment if the probability that it is contained in any given interval is proportional to the length of that interval. Without going into the general theory of measure, let us merely point out that as a result of this definition the probability that a point (restricted to the interval from 0 to 1) is contained in a set consisting of a finite or countable infinite number of nonoverlapping intervals equals the sum of the lengths of the intervals. If the intervals overlap, the probability is less than this sum. Let us apply this to the rational points p/q contained in the interval from 0 to 1. The point p/q is contained in the interval

$$\frac{p}{q} \pm \frac{\alpha}{q^3}$$

whose length is $2\alpha/q^3$, where α is an arbitrary positive constant. The number of intervals of this form for a given value of q is less than q, since p is an integer less than q and relatively prime to q. Thus, the total sum of the intervals is less than

$$2\alpha \sum_2^\infty \frac{1}{q^2}$$

and it can be made as small as one wants by choosing α sufficiently small. It follows that the probability of randomly selecting a rational number on the interval from 0 to 1 is less than any predetermined constant; in other words, it is equal to zero.

The same argument applies to any denumerable set of points on the interval from 0 to 1, for example, to the set of all algebraic numbers. One also obtains denumerable sets by considering all the numbers defined by an infinite series (or continued fraction, etc.), where the law for successive terms is given in such a way that, starting with a given term, they can all be calculated. Since all other processes by which one can define a given number can be written in at most a finite number of words (after all, it is humanly impossible to write more than 10^{10} words), one arrives again at a denumerable set. It follows that the probability is zero that a number chosen at random is one which, starting with the integers, can effectively be defined by some process.

This strange-looking result leads to the question how one can actually select a number at random between 0 and 1, or a point at random on a segment of a given length. It has been tried to represent this choice by imagining a very fine needle with which one picks a point, but it is clear that this procedure is very crude. Physical processes can lead only to approximations, that is, to a point (or number) given only to 7 or 8 decimals. It is only through an abstract algebraic process that one can visualize such a choice, and we shall see to what new difficulties this will lead.

11.4 *The Choice of a Decimal Number*

Since we are accustomed to the decimal notation, it will be convenient to refer to a number written in this notation. If the number is contained between 0 and 1, it is clear that the first digit after the decimal point must be 0, 1, 2, . . . , 8, or 9, depending on whether the corresponding point is contained in the first, second, third, . . . , of the 10 equal intervals into which the interval from 0 to 1 is divided by the points whose abscissas are 0.1, 0.2, . . . , and 0.9.

Thus, in accordance with the definition of a continuous probability, the probability that the first digit after the decimal point is, say, a 7 is equal to 1/10. Similarly, when the first digit after the decimal point is known, the probability that the second digit is, say, a 6 is equal to 1/10, and so on. One can thus obtain a number randomly selected on the interval from 0 to 1 by making a denumerable infinity of successive drawings, analogous to the drawings by which one obtains the digits of a winning lottery ticket. For each drawing, each of the digits from 0 to 9 has the same probability, namely, a probability of 1/10.

It is evident that there can be no question of actually performing a very large number of drawings, particularly an infinite number of drawings. Nevertheless, without actually performing such drawings, one can study certain properties of their results by means of the theory of repeated trials and also the theory of denumerable probabilities. We shall thus study two cases, assuming first that the number of drawings is small enough to be actually performed. Then we shall assume that the drawings are too numerous to be actually made; for the mathematician, this does not rule out the right to pose certain questions and to study related problems.

11.5 *A Finite Number of Drawings*

First, let us suppose that the number of drawings is finite. One can then picture a simple mechanism which makes the drawing and records the result in one second; it can make a million drawings in about a month. In the remainder of this section we shall consider the case where there are 1,000 drawings and, hence, $10^{1,000}$ possible results. This is large enough to permit the application of the law of chance. For example, one could assert that it is impossible for the last n digits (where n is contained between 50 and 500) to duplicate exactly a series of consecutive digits appearing among the first $1,000 - n$ digits drawn. If this were the case, one could assert that the decimal development obtained has a tendency to be periodic, namely, that it might represent a rational number. Of course, there are rational numbers for which the period does not begin until after a great number of nonperiodic digits, or for which the period itself covers more than a thousand digits.

More generally, the number of irrational numbers, defined in a simple way, that have actually been calculated to many decimals is very small. One could thus assert with certainty that the first m digits drawn will not coincide with the corresponding digits for such numbers as π, e, $\sqrt{2}$, and so forth.

Impossibilities like these are brought out even more clearly if one substitutes for the decimal notation an alphabetic notation, where the digits are the 26 letters of the alphabet. In this way, a number which has 1,000 digits after the decimal point in the decimal notation would be equivalent to a number having barely more than 500 letters in the alphabetic notation. If the letters are drawn at random, one could assert that one will never obtain a text of 500 words appearing anywhere in the National Library, or even in all newspapers which have appeared or will appear throughout this century. The number of such texts certainly does not exceed 10^{10}, and the probability of duplicating one of them is thus $10^{10} \cdot 10^{-1,000} = 10^{-900}$. It would be equally unlikely to obtain a sequence of letters making any sense whatsoever. Among the decimal numbers that one will surely not get by virtue of the law of chance are, for example, those in which 50 consecutive digits are all alike, those in which the digit 7 appears fewer than 20 or more than 200 times, and so on.

Persons buying lottery tickets often refuse to buy tickets with very unusual numbers, say, 555,555. They are under the impression that this number will not win, which is correct in the sense that the probability of its winning is 1 in a million and, hence, negligible from the human perspective. In other words, it would be entirely unreasonable to count on winning with the ticket in order to pay a debt or do business. However, the person buying the ticket is in error in assuming that the ticket 141,592 has a better chance than the ticket 555,555. The two outcomes are equiprobable (or better, equally improbable), and in case the reader is familiar with the decimal expansion of π, he will agree that 141,592 is even more special, or more peculiar, than 555,555. Had we considered 100 digits rather than 6 digits, the probabilities would have been negligible from the supercosmic perspective, and we can assert that we will obtain a number consisting of 100 consecutive fives or the first 100 digits of the decimal expansion of π. If one actually performs the drawings, the number one obtains is, of course, *a priori* as unlikely as any other 100-digit number; this is no paradox, since the number was not specified in advance and some number *has* to be obtained. Similarly, if one randomly selects 100 letters of the alphabet, one *must* obtain some particular sequence of 100 letters; what is improbable is that the 100 letters will constitute a phrase which is meaningful in a given language. It is similarly improbable that the 100 digits obtained belong to those sequences which are considered "special" by mathematicians.

If, then, to choose a number on the interval from 0 to 1, one actually draws a great number of digits, one can be certain that the digits thus obtained will not follow any given rule that is either obvious, as in the case of a repeating decimal, or hidden, as in the case of decimal expansion of e or π. There is thus no chance that after one has made 1,000 drawings one will be led to believe that one has obtained (as nearly as possible) a simple rational number or a known irrational number such as e, π, $\sqrt{2}$, etc. In fact, a mathematician would be as bewildered by such a number as a reader would be by a sequence of 1,000 letters. It is extremely improbable that he would be able to indicate any property connected in any way with a mathematical theory concerning given numbers.

11.6 *An Infinite Number of Drawings*

The whole matter appears in an entirely different light if one considers an infinite number of drawings; it is no longer a question concerning the law of chance, as it is assumed that no obstacles are presented by numbers which are too large to be accessible.

We know, by virtue of the application of the law of large numbers to infinitely many repeated trials, that the relative frequency of each of the digits $0, 1, \ldots, 9$ has the limit $1/10$, and that it approaches this limit very rapidly. It is clear, however, that instead of drawing from among the 10 digits in the decimal notation one could also draw from among the 100 combinations $00, 01, \ldots, 98, 99$, or from among the 1,000 combinations obtained by taking three digits at a time. If follows that if one is given a set of n arbitrary digits, one can assert that *no matter how large n might be* the set has the same relative frequency as each of the 10^n possible sets of n digits. Thus, a set of 1,000 consecutive fives is not impossible, but it has the same relative frequency as each of the $10^{1,000}$ sets of 1,000 digits. It would hardly seem necessary to point out to the reader that to be able to write these $10^{1,000}$ sets of 1,000 digits it would not even suffice to fill the universe with reams of paper having the thickness of an atom, while using symbols which themselves are as small as an atom. This would accomodate only a small portion of all these numbers. We are thus dealing with theoretical spectulations, analogous in a certain sense to spectulations concerning infinite geometrical figures, imaginary figures, or multidimensional spaces.

Decimal numbers are referred to as *normal* if the relative frequency for each of the 10 digits tends to $1/10$, and as *absolutely normal with respect to the base 10* if the same property holds for each set of *n* consecutive digits (that is, if their relative frequencies tend to 10^{-n}). One could strengthen these definitions by demanding that a normal number must not only satisfy the preceding conditions, but all the conditions one might derive from the calculus of probability for a decimal number whose successive digits are drawn by lot. This has the disadvantage that it is rather vague, and it would seem preferable to return to the simpler definition given above; when necessary, the definition may be supplemented with further conditions.

One can also define normal numbers with reference to bases other than 10, and a number which is normal with respect to all bases of enumeration is called absolutely normal.

It is easy to show that the set of numbers which are not normal with respect to a given base has measure zero, and it also follows from the elementary theory of measure that the set of absolutely normal numbers on the interval from 0 to 1 has measure 1; this means that a point chosen at random on the interval from 0 to 1 has a probability of 1 of being an absolutely normal number. On the basis of these results, Henri Lebesgue "named" these numbers absolutely normal, distinguishing between "naming" and "defining." In other words, an absolutely normal number has not been defined in the same precise manner as, for example, such numbers as e, π, $\sqrt{2}$, log 7, etc. It would be interesting to try and demonstrate that a specific number, perhaps one of those just given, is actually absolutely normal. Such a result would clarify a good deal about the theory of normal numbers, which so far consists mainly of the general definitions of these numbers. It would seem that most mathematicians would agree to the proposition that numbers such as e, π, and $\sqrt{2}$ are absolutely normal, but they would be equally inclined to agree that a rigorous demonstration of this proposition would be extremely difficult.

It is known that quadratic numbers are not normal by virtue of the algorithm for continued fractions; their development as continued fractions is periodic. So far as algebraic numbers are concerned, the theorem of Lionville imposes a limitation on the values of the incomplete quotients of a given rank, so that their development as continued fractions cannot be regarded as absolutely normal either. It has also been known for a long time that certain expressions in e and π obey simple laws when expanded as continued fractions. The question of normal expansions in continued fractions, as they are defined by probabilistic considerations, is thus simpler than that of normal expansions in the decimal notation or in other systems of enumeration with a fixed base. On the other hand, it is known that the number e has a specially simple expansion in a system of enumeration with a factorial base. We shall have to be satisfied with having posed these problems, without being able to indicate the methods of research by which they might be solved.

11.7 *Generalization of the Problem of Choice*

We have seen the difficulties posed by the problem of randomly choosing a number from a continuous set. The difficulties are even greater if one wants to choose infinitely many numbers and their possible combinations. For the study of problems of this kind, some of which are related to the axiom of choice of Zermelo, I must refer to some of my other writings, mainly to my *Elements of the Theory of Sets*. Indeed, the theory of continuous probabilities has many analogies with the theory of the measure of sets, and in the study of certain questions one can sometimes employ the language of measure and sometimes the language of probability. Let me refer again to the book mentioned above, especially to Note II on probabilities in denumerable sets.

PART THREE

Probabilities of Causes

CHAPTER TWELVE

The Discrete Case

12.1 *Some Simple Problems*

PROBLEM 38. *Urn A contains 3 white balls and 1 black ball, and urn B contains 1 white ball and 3 black balls. If one ball is drawn from one of the urns, chosen at random, and it is observed to be white, what is the probability that it came from urn A?*

Since the two urns contain the same number of balls, the probability of drawing any one of the eight balls is the same. There are 3 white balls in A, 1 in B, and the probability that the white ball came from A is, therefore, 3/4; this is the required probability.

One might also argue as follows: Imagine 40 pairs of urns A_1, A_2, ..., A_{40}, B_1, B_2, ..., B_{40}, where each urn A_i has the same composition as urn A and each urn B_i has the same composition as urn B. Suppose that one urn is randomly selected from each pair and that a ball is drawn from each of these urns. If 20 of the urns chosen have the composition of urn A and 20 have the composition of urn B, the most likely result is that the former will yield 15 white balls and 5 black balls while the latter will yield 5 white balls and 15 black balls. One thus obtains the following:

20 drawings from A yield 15 white balls and 5 black balls
20 drawings from B yield 5 white balls and 15 black balls

___

40 drawings   yield 20 white balls and 20 black balls

It can be seen from this table that among the 20 drawings furnishing the white balls 15 came from urns like A and 5 came from urns like B; hence, the probability that any one of the white balls came from an urn having the composition of A is $3/4$.

PROBLEM 39. *Urns A and B have the same composition as in the preceding problem. Two balls are drawn in succession from one of the urns, chosen at random, and the first ball is replaced before the second is drawn so as not to disturb the composition of the urn. If both balls drawn are white, what is the probability that they came from urn A?*

The probability of drawing two white balls from urn A is $9/16$ and the corresponding probability for urn B is $1/16$. Thus, if one repeats the experiment 32 times, drawing 16 times from urn A and 16 times from urn B, the most likely result would be to obtain two white balls in the ratio of 9 to 1. It follows that there are 9 chances in 10 that the two white balls came from urn A. More generally, if n consecutive drawings (with replacement) all yielded white balls, the odds are 3^n to 1 that they came from urn A.

PROBLEM 40. *Each of three chests has two drawers. The first chest has a gold coin in each drawer, the second chest has a gold coin in one drawer and a silver coin in the other drawer, while the third chest has a silver coin in each drawer. If one opens one of the drawers and finds a gold coin, what is the probability that the second drawer of this chest will also contain a gold coin?*

The question reduces to the following: What is the probability that the drawer which was opened belongs to the first chest? Since three of the drawers contain gold coins, each has a probability of $1/3$; the required probability is thus $2/3$, since two of the three drawers belong to the first chest.

PROBLEM 41. *Among 10 urns there is one, urn A, which contains 5 white balls and 1 black ball, while each of the other urns, urns B, contains 2 white balls and 2 black balls. If one ball is drawn at random from one of the urns and it is observed to be white, what is the probability that it came from urn A?*

One cannot reason here as simply as in the preceding problems, since the urns B do not contain the same number of balls as urn A. However, using the least common multiple, one can reduce the problem to the previous case. Nothing would be changed if one doubled the number of balls in A, preserving their proportion, and if one similarly tripled the number of balls in each urn B. Urn A would then contain 10 white balls and 2 black balls, while each urn B would contain 6 white balls and 6 black balls. There would thus be $10 + 6 \cdot 9 = 64$ white balls, of which 10 are in urn A; it follows that the probability that the white ball came from urn A is $10/64 = 5/32$.

12.2 *The Formula of Bayes*

Consider n urns among which n_1, called urns A_1, have the same proportion p_1 of white balls, n_2, called urns A_2, have the same proportion p_2 of white balls, ..., and n_k, called urns A_k, have the same proportion p_k of white balls. The $n = n_1 + n_2 + ... + n_k$ urns are otherwise identical, and one ball is drawn at random from one of these urns. If the ball drawn is white, what is the probability that it came from one of the urns A_1?

Suppose that each urn contains N balls, so that each of the urns A_1 contains p_1N white balls,* each of the urns A_2 contains p_2N white balls, etc. It follows that the total number of white balls is

$$n_1p_1N + n_2p_2N + ... + n_kp_kN$$

among which n_1p_1N come from one of the urns A_1. Hence, the probability that the white ball came from one of the urns A_1 is

$$P_1 = \frac{n_1p_1N}{n_1p_1N + ... + n_kp_kN} = \frac{n_1p_1}{n_1p_1 + n_2p_2 + ... + n_kp_k}$$

Letting $n_1 = w_1n$, $n_2 = w_2n$, ..., and $n_k = w_kn$, this formula can also be written as

$$P_1 = \frac{p_1w_1}{p_1w_1 + p_2w_2 + ... + p_kw_k}$$

where the significance of the numbers w_i is easily explained.

If one randomly selects one of the urns, the probability of obtaining one of the urns A_1 is w_1, since w_1 is the ratio of n_1 (the number of urns A_1) to n (the total number of urns). One might thus call w_1 the *a priori probability* (that is, prior to the drawing) of choosing an urn of the kind A_1; the probability P_1 we have calculated is correspondingly called the *a posteriori probability*, and the formula for P_1 is called the *formula of Bayes*. It can be derived by using the following argument, which makes use of the theorems for total and composite probabilities.

The probability that the ball drawn is white and that it comes from A_1 can be evaluated in two ways, depending on the order in which one satisfies the two conditions that (1) the ball is white, and (2) it comes from A_1.

(1) The probability that the ball is white is a total probability since the white ball can come from one of the urns A_1, from one of the urns A_2, etc.; hence, the value of this probability is

$$p_1w_1 + p_2w_2 + ... + p_kw_k$$

On the other hand, the probability that a ball comes from A_1 *given that it is white* was denoted P_1, and it follows that the required probability is

$$P_1(p_1w_1 + p_2w_2 + ... + p_kw_k)$$

---

* It is assumed that the number N is chosen so that p_1N, p_2N, ..., and p_kN are all integers.

(2) The probability that the ball comes from A_1 is w_1, and the probability that it is white *given that it comes from A_1* is p_1. Hence, the required probability is

$$p_1 w_1$$

and, equating the two results, we obtain the formula of Bayes. This derivation holds regardless of the events to which the probabilities refer. What makes the application of the formula difficult at times is the problem of obtaining values for the *a priori* probabilities. Let us consider some examples.

PROBLEM 42. *Several drawings are made (with replacement) from an urn A containing an unknown number of white and black balls. If the balls drawn include r white balls and s black balls, what is the most probable composition of the urn?*

One might be tempted to reply that the most probable composition is the one where the ratio of the number of white balls to the number of black balls is r to s, but this would not be correct unless one made assumptions about the a *priori* probabilities which are not only very special, but which would have to vary with the values of r and s. This is illustrated by means of the following special cases.

(1) Suppose that the urn contains 6 balls and that $r = 2$ and $s = 0$, namely, that two successive drawings yielded two white balls. There are seven possibilities concerning the composition of the urn which we shall denote $A_0, A_1, \ldots,$ and A_6, where A_k represents the case where the urn contains $6 - k$ white balls and k black balls. The table which follows contains the probability of obtaining two white balls in a row for each of the seven possibilities:

A_0 6 white and 0 black $p_0 = 1$

A_1 5 white and 1 black $p_1 = \left(\dfrac{5}{6}\right)^2 = \dfrac{25}{36}$

A_2 4 white and 2 black $p_2 = \left(\dfrac{4}{6}\right)^2 = \dfrac{16}{36}$

A_3 3 white and 3 black $p_3 = \left(\dfrac{3}{6}\right)^2 = \dfrac{9}{36}$

A_4 2 white and 4 black $p_4 = \left(\dfrac{2}{6}\right)^2 = \dfrac{4}{36}$

A_5 1 white and 5 black $p_5 = \left(\dfrac{1}{6}\right)^2 = \dfrac{1}{36}$

A_6 0 white and 6 black $p_6 = 0$

Designating the *a priori* probabilities of these seven cases as w_1, w_2, ..., and w_6, we find that their *a posteriori* probabilities P_0, P_1, ..., and P_6 are given by

$$P_0 = \frac{36w_0}{36w_0 + 25w_1 + 16w_2 + 9w_3 + 4w_4 + w_5}$$

$$P_1 = \frac{25w_1}{36w_0 + 25w_1 + 16w_2 + 9w_3 + 4w_4 + w_5}$$

. . . .

$$P_5 = \frac{w_5}{36w_0 + 25w_1 + 16w_2 + 9w_3 + 4w_4 + w_5}$$

$$P_6 = 0$$

It is apparent from these formulas that we can specify w_0, w_1, ..., and w_5 in such a way that P_0, P_1, ..., and P_5 will assume any arbitrary set of values whose sum equals 1. (P_6 must equal zero, for if one draws white balls it is certain that the balls cannot all be black.)

To complete the solution of the problem, one must thus make some assumption concerning the values of w_0, w_1, ..., and w_5. One plausible possibility is to assume that the *a priori* probabilities are all equal, namely, that one randomly selects one of seven urns having, respectively, the seven possible compositions. This would give

$$P_0 = \tfrac{36}{91}, \quad P_1 = \tfrac{25}{91}, \quad P_2 = \tfrac{16}{91}, \quad P_3 = \tfrac{9}{91}, \quad P_4 = \tfrac{4}{91}, \quad P_5 = \tfrac{1}{91}, \quad P_6 = 0$$

Another possibility is to assume that the urn has been filled at random by means of successive drawings (with replacement) from an urn containing the same number of white balls as black balls. By virtue of Pascal's triangle, one obtains

$$w_0 = w_6 = \tfrac{1}{64}, \quad w_1 = w_5 = \tfrac{6}{64}, \quad w_2 = w_4 = \tfrac{15}{64}, \quad w_3 = \tfrac{20}{64}$$

and, hence,

$$P_0 = \tfrac{6}{112}, \quad P_1 = \tfrac{25}{112}, \quad P_2 = \tfrac{40}{112}, \quad P_3 = \tfrac{30}{112}, \quad P_4 = \tfrac{10}{112}, \quad P_5 = \tfrac{1}{112},$$

$$P_6 = 0$$

It can be seen that this result differs considerably from the preceding one. The most probable alternative is now that the urn contains 4 white balls and 2 black balls, since the *a priori* probability of this alternative is much greater than that of the alternative that the balls are all white.

Let us suppose now that $r = s = 1,000$, namely, that 2,000 drawings have yielded as many white balls as black balls, and let us look for the probability that the proportion of white balls in the urn is p. (The proportion of black balls is correspondingly $q = 1 - p$.) If p is the true proportion, the expected number of white balls is 2,000p and the observed deviation is

$$2,000p - 1,000 = 1,000(2p - 1)$$

Since the unit deviation is

$$\sqrt{4,000pq} = 20\sqrt{10pq}$$

the relative deviation λ is

$$\lambda = \frac{1,000(2p - 1)}{20\sqrt{10pq}} = 50\frac{(2p - 1)}{\sqrt{10pq}}$$

and it is known that the probability of λ exceeding 5 is very small. Such a large value of λ can thus be ignored, unless the corresponding *a priori* probability is very high. Letting $p = \frac{1}{2} + \alpha$ and $q = \frac{1}{2} - \alpha$, and ignoring terms in α^2, one obtains

$$\lambda = \frac{200\alpha}{\sqrt{10}} = 20\alpha\sqrt{10}$$

and it can be seen that λ exceeds $\sqrt{10}$ when α exceeds $1/20$. Let us now suppose that the *a priori* probability of α assuming a value between $-1/20$ and $1/20$ is proportional to the length of the corresponding interval. Thus, the probability that one observes a relative deviation λ between $20\alpha\sqrt{10}$ and $20\alpha\sqrt{10} + d\lambda$, given that α is contained between α and $\alpha + d\alpha$, is

$$\frac{1}{\sqrt{\pi}} e^{-4,000\alpha^2} d\lambda$$

The probability that α is contained between α and $\alpha + d\alpha$ is thus

$$\frac{\dfrac{1}{\sqrt{\pi}} e^{-4,000\alpha^2} d\alpha}{\dfrac{1}{\sqrt{\pi}} \displaystyle\int_{-1/20}^{1/20} e^{-4,000\alpha^2} d\alpha} = \sqrt{4,000}e^{-4,000\alpha^2} d\alpha$$

where the limits of integration in the denominator can be put equal to $-\infty$ and $+\infty$ without introducing an appreciable error.

The probability that the proportion of white balls is contained between 0.500 and 0.501 is obtained by substituting $\alpha = 0$ and $d\alpha = 0.001$, which gives

$$\frac{\sqrt{4,000}}{1,000} = \frac{2\sqrt{10}}{100}$$

Similarly, the probability that the proportion is contained between 0.510 and 0.511 is obtained by substituting $\alpha = 0.01$ and $d\alpha = 0.001$, which gives

$$\frac{\sqrt{4,000}}{1,000} e^{-0.4}$$

Finally, the probability that the proportion is contained between 0.525 and 0.526 is obtained by substituting $\alpha = 1/40$ and $d\alpha = 0.001$, which gives

$$\frac{\sqrt{4,000}}{1,000} e^{-2.5}$$

and this is about 10 times smaller than the preceding value.

(2) Let us now suppose that $r = 10$, $s = 0$, and that the urn has been filled by means of 800 random drawings from another urn having as many white balls as black balls. The *a priori* probability for the urn to contain $400 + h$ white balls is

$$\frac{1}{40\sqrt{\pi}} e^{-h^2/400}$$

since the unit deviation equals 20. In order to determine the most probable composition of the urn, let us observe that the probability of getting 10 white balls in 10 drawings is

$$\left(\frac{400 + h}{800}\right)^{10}$$

so that we must find the maximum value of the product

$$\frac{1}{40\sqrt{\pi}} e^{-h^2/400} \left(\frac{400 + h}{800}\right)^{10}$$

Except for a constant, the logarithm of this quantity is

$$10 \cdot \log\left(1 + \frac{h}{400}\right) - \frac{h^2}{400}$$

and equating to zero its derivative with respect to h, we obtain

$$\frac{10}{400 + h} - \frac{h}{200} = 0, \qquad h^2 + 400h - 2,000 = 0$$

$$h = -200 + \sqrt{42,000} = 200[-1 + \sqrt{1 + 1/20}] = 5 \quad \text{(approximately)}$$

Hence, the most probable composition is 405 white balls and 395 black balls, and it should be observed that drawing 10 white balls in a row does not add much to the likelihood of a greater difference in the composition of the urn. In other words, owing to the manner in which the urn was filled, it is very improbable that the number of white balls in the urn is much greater than the number of black balls.

The situation would have been different if 100 consecutive drawings (with replacement) had all yielded white balls. If this actually happened, one should first investigate whether there is not some error in the experiment; such a result is extremely unlikely. If the results are acceptable, one has to maximize the expression

$$100 \cdot \log{(400 + h)} - \frac{h^2}{400}$$

and this gives

$$\frac{100}{400 + h} - \frac{h}{400} = 0, \qquad h^2 + 400h - 20,000 = 0$$

$$h = -200 + \sqrt{60,000} = 44 \quad \text{(approximately)}$$

12.3 *Applications*

There are situations where the evaluation of the *a priori* probabilities is simply a matter of estimation and the results will, of course, depend on the values of the estimates. The following is a classical example.

PROBLEM 43. *Peter plays Écarté with a stranger who turns up a king the first time he has the deal. What is the probability that the stranger is a professional cheat?*

In the solution which Poincaré gave this problem he assumed implicitly that a professional cheat would turn up a king every time he has the chance. Although I have no personal experience in this matter (and neither did Poincaré), it would seem to me that this assumption is not very likely. An honest player turns up a king on the average $1/8$ of the time, and it would seem that someone who has such "good luck" each time would rapidly cause suspicion. It would seem more reasonable to estimate the probability that a cheat will turn up a king, say, as $1/4$, whereas for an honest player this same probability is $1/8$.

Let us designate by w the *a priori* probability that Peter's adversary is a cheat. The *a priori* probability that he is honest is thus $1 - w$, and the *a posteriori* probability P that he is a cheat (after he has turned up a king) is

$$P = \frac{\frac{1}{4}w}{\frac{1}{4}w + \frac{1}{8}(1 - w)} = \frac{2w}{1 + w}$$

If $w = 1/2$, namely, if there is a fifty-fifty chance that Peter's adversary is a cheat, one obtains $P = 2/3$, and this shows that the single observation has modified the probability to quite an extent. However, it should also be noted that it would be very imprudent of Peter to play with an opponent of whose morality he has such a low opinion. The fact that Peter is willing to play suggests that he regards w as being very small. If w is small, P differs very little from $2w$, and in any event it is less than $2w$, that is, the probability is less than doubled by the observed event. If Peter's partner is such that $w = 1/100,000$, then $P = 1/50,000$, that is, P is practically as negligible as w. If Peter is sure of his partner and assumes that $w = 0$, then P is also equal to 0; in other words, the observed event does not shake his confidence. It would seem that the results we have obtained conform with common sense.

PROBLEM 44. *An examiner has prepared 10 written questions, one of which is to be drawn at random by each candidate. Among two candidates, the more intelligent one can answer 9 of these 10 questions correctly, while the other can answer only one. If one of these canditates draws a question he can answer, what is the probability that he is the more intelligent one?*

If the *a priori* probability is 1/2, the *a posteriori* probability is

$$P = \frac{\frac{1}{2} \cdot \frac{9}{10}}{\frac{1}{2} \cdot \frac{9}{10} + \frac{1}{2} \cdot \frac{1}{10}} = \frac{9}{10}$$

PROBLEM 45. *One class of 20 students contains 10 good students, 5 average students, and 5 poor students, while another class of 20 students contains 5 good students, 5 average students, and 10 poor students. If someone examines one student selected at random from each class and finds the student from class A superior to the one from class B, what is the probability that class A is the first of the two?*

If one randomly selects one student from each class, there are $10 \cdot 15 + 5 \cdot 10 = 200$ combinations in which the student from the first class is the better one. Also, there are $10 \cdot 5 + 5 \cdot 5 + 5 \cdot 10 = 125$ combinations in which the two students belong to the same category, and $5 \cdot 10 + 5 \cdot 5 = 75$ combinations in which the student from the second class is the better one. If the *a priori* probabilities are 1/2 and 1/2, the probability that class A is the first one is

$$\frac{\frac{1}{2} \cdot 200}{\frac{1}{2} \cdot 200 + \frac{1}{2} \cdot 75} = \frac{8}{11}$$

In the case where one examines two students from each class and each student from class A is superior to the corresponding student from class B, the probability that class A is the first one is

$$\frac{\frac{1}{2}(200)^2}{\frac{1}{2}(200)^2 + \frac{1}{2}(75)^2} = \frac{64}{73}$$

This illustrates how replication adds to the chances of drawing the correct conclusion. It is assumed, of course, that one does not make any errors of judgement, as has been assumed throughout the solution of this problem.

PROBLEM 46. *In a regiment some soldiers have served for one year, some have served for two years, and some for three years. If two soldiers are selected at random and one of them has served longer than the other, what is the probability that he has served for three years?*

Let a be the number of soldiers who have served for one year, b the number of soldiers who have served for two years, and c the number of soldiers who have served for three years. Given one soldier who has served two years and another soldier selected at random, the probability that the first soldier has served longer than the second is

$$\frac{a}{a+b+c-1}$$

since the second soldier is one of the $a+b+c-1$ who remain after the first soldier has been selected, and since among these there are a favorable cases. Similarly, the probability that a soldier who has served for three years is older than a second soldier selected at random is

$$\frac{a+b}{a+b+c-1}$$

On the other hand, the *a priori* probabilities of selecting a soldier who has served two years or three years are, respectively,*

$$\frac{b}{a+b+c} \quad \text{and} \quad \frac{c}{a+b+c}$$

and the *a posteriori* probability that the soldier who has served longer has served for three years is

$$\frac{\dfrac{c}{a+b+c} \cdot \dfrac{a+b}{a+b+c-1}}{\dfrac{c}{a+b+c} \cdot \dfrac{a+b}{a+b+c-1} + \dfrac{b}{a+b+c} \cdot \dfrac{a}{a+b+c-1}}$$

namely

$$\frac{c(a+b)}{c(a+b)+ab} = 1 - \frac{ab}{bc+ca+ab}$$

This probability can also be written in the form

$$\frac{\dfrac{1}{a}+\dfrac{1}{b}}{\dfrac{1}{a}+\dfrac{1}{b}+\dfrac{1}{c}}$$

---

* There is no need to consider the case where the first soldier has served only one year since this would make it impossible for him to have served longer than the other soldier,

If $a = b = c$, the probability is 2/3; if $a = 2b = 4c$, that is, if each year has half as many as the preceding year, the probability is

$$\frac{\frac{1}{4} + \frac{1}{2}}{\frac{1}{4} + \frac{1}{2} + 1} = \frac{3}{7}$$

which is less than 1/2. In this case it would be advantageous to bet that the soldier who has served longer has served two years, since there are twice as many of those as there are soldiers who have served three years, and twice as many who have served one year as there are soldiers who have served two years.

CHAPTER THIRTEEN

Statistical Problems

13.1 *The Concept of Statistical Probabilities*

The study of certain statistics has shown that there exist relatively constant ratios in the numerical description of various phenomena. For example, the proportion of male births to the number of inhabitants does not vary much in a given region over a given period, when they are observed over several successive years (not including years of war or years immediately following a war). Of course, such a phenomenon is not *a priori* comparable to drawings from an urn containing a given proportion of white balls; the only analogy that is immediately apparent between the two phenomena is the constancy of a certain ratio. These ratios, and others like them, have been evaluated to a sufficient degree of approximation to give them the name of *statistical probabilities*. It is important to note that the difference between statistical probabilities and abstract and rigorously defined probabilities is of the same nature as that between geometrical figures and their physical counterparts, say, the difference between a sphere and an orange.

13.2 *Male and Female Births*

One of the statistical probabilities which has been studied for the longest time, and whose constancy is remarkable, is the probability that a newborn baby is a boy. It has been known for quite some time that this probability is slightly greater than 1/2; that is, the number of male births is slightly greater than the number of female births. We shall not attempt to review here all the research that has been done on this question, but we shall

132

indicate how the problem may be phrased in rigorous terms and how one might look for a solution.

Suppose that it has been established, over a long period of time, that in a given country the ratio of male births to the total number of births is $1/2 + \alpha$, and hence that the ratio of female births to the total number of births is $1/2 - \alpha$.* The ratio of the number of male births to the number of female births is thus

$$\frac{1/2 + \alpha}{1/2 - \alpha} = 1 + 4\alpha + 8\alpha^2 + \ldots$$

where the value of α is generally close to 0.01 and does not exceed 0.015. Hence, the term in α^2 is usually negligible for the degree of approximation justified by the observations one has at one's disposal.

The following question suggests itself first. Suppose the coefficient α has been calculated by averaging data covering, say, 20 years, and that for each year of this period one calculates what the number of male births *should have been* by multiplying the total number of births by $1/2 + \alpha$. The numbers thus obtained can be expected to differ from the observed values, *but can one say that the errors satisfy the same laws as if each birth had been drawn from an urn containing N balls of which $(1/2 + \alpha)N$ are white?* If one actually made n drawings from such an urn, the most probable number of white balls would be $(1/2 + \alpha)n$ and the unit deviation would be

$$\sqrt{2npq} = \sqrt{2n\left(\frac{1}{2} + \alpha\right)\left(\frac{1}{2} - \alpha\right)} = \sqrt{\frac{n}{2} - 2n\alpha^2}$$

Since the square of α is assumed to be very small, one can ignore the term in α^2 without introducing an appreciable error.

One could proceed by calculating the relative deviations, dividing the absolute deviation by the unit deviation, and then investigating whether these relative deviations follow the law of Laplace.

Let us merely indicate here that the verification has been quite satisfactory and that one can conclude, at least as a first approximation, that the analogy to the drawings from an urn is legitimate. We shall accept this result provisionally, and we shall see how other statistical observations will lead to some modifications.

13.3 *The Study of Twins*

It has been observed for a long time that twins are more frequently of the same sex than two nontwins born to the same family. Statistical observations provide the number of twin births consisting of two boys (BB), two

---

* The figures will differ somewhat depending on whether one includes stillbirths. Also, they will not be exactly the same for legitimate and illegitimate births. It seems prudent, at least so far as the older data are concerned, to limit oneself to legitimate living births; this should promise a higher degree of exactitude.

girls (GG), or one boy and one girl (BG), and we shall designate the corresponding statistical probabilities a, b, and c, where $a + b + c = 1$. Once the values of a, b, and c are known, one can solve problems such as the following with reference to the past (and not necessarily the future).

PROBLEM 47. *Given that one of a set of twins is a boy, what is the probability that the other one is also a boy?*

This problem is similar to the problem of the three chests (Problem 40), except that we now have $a \cdot N$ cases BB and $c \cdot N$ cases BG instead of a single chest with two gold coins and a single chest with one gold coin and one silver coin. Hence, the probability is $2a/(2a + c)$.

Actually, this is not the problem whose solution is of the greatest interest. The question that arises is how one can know when the sex of one of the children can be regarded as having as its *cause* the sex of the other. The main difficulty is to formulate this problem in a precise way, and in order to accomplish this it will be necessary to give it an entirely objective formulation, that is, independent of all physiological interpretations. This can be done in several ways, of which we shall arbitrarily select the following.

PROBLEM 48. *A certain number of series of two successive drawings are made from an urn containing, in a given proportion, balls marked* B *and balls marked* G. *Each drawing is written down by an assistant, who records* BB, BG, GB, *or* GG, *depending on the case, but he is sometimes inattentive and in that case, instead of recording the second letter correctly, he records for it the same letter as the first. Given the records kept by the assistant, it is desired to determine in what proportion of the cases he was inattentive.*

It will be assumed that the results are given as in the following kind of table:

BB	aN
GG	bN
BG + GB	cN

where N is the total number of drawings. Designating by $1/2 + \alpha$ the proportion of balls marked B and by λ the proportion of the cases where the assistant was inattentive, one obtains the three relations

$$(1 - \lambda)(\tfrac{1}{2} + \alpha)^2 + \lambda(\tfrac{1}{2} + \alpha) = a$$

$$(1 - \lambda)(\tfrac{1}{2} - \alpha)^2 + \lambda(\tfrac{1}{2} - \alpha) = b$$

$$2(1 - \lambda)(\tfrac{1}{2} + \alpha)(\tfrac{1}{2} - \alpha) = c$$

which reduce to two since $a + b + c = 1$.

If one assumes that α is given and that λ is the only unknown, the problem cannot be solved unless the numbers a, b, and c are such that $2\alpha = a - b$, a relationship which is obtained by subtracting the second equation from the first equation. We shall assume that this condition is satisfied and it follows that the system reduces to the first equation (or the second). A more symmetrical equation can be obtained by adding the two term by term, which gives

$$\tfrac{1}{2}(1 - \lambda) + 2\alpha^2 + \lambda = a + b$$

or, ignoring α^2,

$$\lambda = 2a + 2b - 1$$

Making use of the relation $a + b + c = 1$, one can also write

$$\lambda = a + b - c = 1 - 2c$$

and the most convenient formula in actual practice is

$$\lambda = \frac{aN + bN - cN}{N}$$

For example, 1905 statistics for France gave

BB	$aN = 2{,}933$
GG	$bN = 2{,}797$
BG	$cN = 3{,}188$

and one concludes that

$$\lambda = \frac{2{,}542}{8{,}918} = 0.28 \ldots$$

namely, that everything happened as if approximately 28 per cent of the time the sex of the second child was determined by the sex of the first.

13.4 *Births in the Same Family*

Analogous investigations could be made on consecutive births in the same family, but unfortunately statistical records are too scarce to permit a thorough study of this question. The statistics one has can best be utilized by means of the following artifact: Assuming that the probability of a male birth is always $1/2 + \alpha$, the probabilities of the four alternatives BB, BG, GB, and GG are, respectively,

BB:	$(\tfrac{1}{2} + \alpha)^2 = \tfrac{1}{4} + \alpha + \alpha^2$
BG:	$(\tfrac{1}{2} + \alpha)(\tfrac{1}{2} - \alpha) = \tfrac{1}{4} - \alpha^2$
GB:	$(\tfrac{1}{2} - \alpha)(\tfrac{1}{2} + \alpha) = \tfrac{1}{4} - \alpha^2$
GG:	$(\tfrac{1}{2} - \alpha)^2 = \tfrac{1}{4} - \alpha + \alpha^2$

It follows that

$$\frac{BB + GG}{BG + GB} = \frac{\frac{1}{2} + 2\alpha^2}{\frac{1}{2} - 2\alpha^2} = \frac{1 + 4\alpha^2}{1 - 4\alpha^2} = 1 + 8\alpha^2 + \ldots$$

Since the value of α is always assumed to be close to 0.01, the ratio thus obtained differs from unity by at most 0.001. Furthermore, if one assumes that the population on which the figures are based consists of several subpopulations for which α has the values $\alpha_1, \alpha_2, \ldots, \alpha_k$, the value of the above ratio would be

$$\frac{n_1(1 + 4\alpha_1^2) + n_2(1 + 4\alpha_2^2) + \ldots + n_k(1 + 4\alpha_k^2)}{n_1(1 - 4\alpha_1^2) + n_2(1 - 4\alpha_2^2) + \ldots + n_k(1 - 4\alpha_k^2)}$$

where $n_1, n_2, \ldots$, and n_k are the number of observations from the respective subpopulations. This ratio differs from unity by less than $8\alpha^2$, where α denotes the largest of the numbers $\alpha_1, \alpha_2, \ldots$, and α_k. If the ratio we have calculated, namely,

$$\frac{BB + GG}{BG + GB}$$

is appreciably greater than 1, one can conclude with some assurance that there are cases where the sex of the second child is determined by that of the first. We shall not attempt to estimate this degree of assurance, since, as we have said earlier, statistical records are not extensive enough to eliminate the small random errors which cannot be avoided when one deals with small numbers.

13.5 Mortality Statistics

If one examines mortality statistics for a given region covering a number of successive years, one is immediately struck by the size of the fluctuations. For example, for the years 1887 through 1906 the number of deaths in France were as shown in the following table.*

Number of Deaths (thousands)		Number of Deaths (thousands)	
1887	843	1897	751
1888	838	1898	810
1889	795	1899	816
1890	877	1900	853
1891	877	1901	785
1892	876	1902	761
1893	868	1903	754
1894	816	1904	761
1895	852	1905	770
1896	772	1906	780

* The fluctuations would be even greater, of course, if one considered periods including years of war or years immediately following a war.

How does one account for these extensive fluctuations? The first explanation that comes to one's mind is that the population on which the data are based is not homogeneous; evidently, mortality statistics depend on age, sex, social conditions, standard of living, and so forth. However, we know (from Sections 5.5, 5.6, and 5.7) that the consideration of several distinct groups which one regards as one population will tend to diminish, never increase, the relative deviation. One must thus look for another explanation. An analysis of the conditions suggests that the number of deaths is frequently increased by epidemics, periods of extreme heat or severe cold, etc. Such phenomena can account for a great number of simultaneous deaths which cannot be regarded as independent. Looking at things from a purely abstract point of view, there seem to be ties among the balls, so that one cannot draw one ball from an urn without also drawing others. This would justify the existence of greater deviations. Suppose, for the sake of argument, that an urn contains 40,000,000 balls of which 800,000 are black, and that 40 million persons are asked to draw one ball each with replacement. The expected number of black balls would be 800,000 and the unit deviation would be

$$\sqrt{2npq} = \frac{1,000 \cdot 7\sqrt{80}}{50} = 1,260 \quad \text{(approximately)}$$

since $n = 40,000,000$, $p = 1/50$, and $q = 49/50$.

Suppose now that one makes only 40,000 drawings, but that each drawing of a black ball is considered worth 1,000 (black balls). The expected number of black balls drawn would be 800 and, in accordance with the convention, this would represent 800,000 black balls. The unit deviation would be

$$\sqrt{80,000 \cdot \frac{1}{50} \cdot \frac{49}{50}} = \frac{7 \cdot 100\sqrt{8}}{50} = 40 \quad \text{(approximately)}$$

where, in accordance with the convention, each unit corresponds to 1,000 black balls. The unit deviation would thus be equivalent to 40,000 and, hence, a deviation of 40,000 from 800,000 would be looked upon as quite probable. It can thus be seen that this hypothesis can account for considerable deviations. Let us now leave the problem of mortality statistics to which we have been led by the preceding considerations, and let us examine briefly how one might pose the general problem of statistical probability.

13.6 The Model of the Urns

In order to avoid unnecessary verbal complications, let us consider series of observations made from the same number of possible cases, for example, from a constant population. For each series one records the number of times a certain kind of event, called a *success*, has occurred. This terminology is conventional, and the term "success" may apply to a birth, a death, a person having a certain disease, and so on. The observations thus furnish a table showing the number of successes obtained for each series, and it should be recalled that one also knows the total number of possible cases. We can now formulate the general problem of mathematical statistics as follows: *Determine a system of drawings made from urns having a fixed composition, so that the results of a series of drawings, interpreted with the aid of coefficients conveniently selected, lead with a very great likelihood to a table which is identical with the table of observations.*

We shall call this problem the *problem of the model of the urns*. The following typifies the kind of solution it can have: Consider three urns U_1, U_2, and U_3 containing white and black balls, identical in shape, with the proportions of black balls being p_1, p_2, and p_3, respectively. If α_1 drawings made with replacement from U_1 yield n_1 black balls, α_2 drawings made with replacement from U_2 yield n_2 black balls, and α_3 drawings made with replacement from U_3 yield n_3 black balls, the number of successes is given by

$$\lambda_1 n_1 + \lambda_2 n_2 + \lambda_3 n_3$$

where the coefficients λ_1, λ_2, λ_3 as well as the integers α_1, α_2, α_3 and the probabilities p_1, p_2, p_3 define the particular model. In what follows, we shall merely indicate several questions that immediately arise in connection with the general problem of the model of the urns.

(1) *Can the problem be solved?* Since we are dealing with approximations, it is clear that the problem can always be solved provided the number of urns is sufficiently large. On the other hand, such a solution may not be very satisfactory, and in practice it is desirable to reduce the number of urns to a minimum. If only one urn is required the problem under consideration is referred to as *normal*; a specially interesting case is the one where two and only two urns are required.

(2) *Does the problem have a unique solution?* There are, of course, many solutions if one assumes that the number of urns can be very large, but in most cases there is only one *simple solution*, and this is the one to which one attaches particular importance.

(3) *By what method does one obtain solutions?* We shall not be able to go into this question, which has given rise to much research since the work done by Karl Pearson. An equally important question is to know what precision one can expect of a solution when the number of observations is relatively small.

To conclude these brief observations, let us point to the analogy between the form we have given to the problem of the model of the urns and the form of problems arising in mechanics and mathematical physics. There, too, the main question is that of constructing a mathematical model which presents a sufficiently close agreement with reality. With this main question resolved (or at least partially resolved, since there are often several solutions), the role of the mathematician is limited to the study of the properties of the model, and this is a problem of pure mathematics. The comparison of the results thus obtained with experience, and the development of theories which make such comparisons possible, lie outside the domain of mathematics. Thus, the role of mathematics is limited, though very important, and in one's theoretical research one must never lose sight of reality and one must always check new ideas against observations and experience.

CHAPTER FOURTEEN

The Continuous Case

14.1 *A Simple Example*

Consider a game analogous to *heads or tails* played with a solid polyhedron having some faces painted white and others painted black. It is tossed into the air and one observes whether it ultimately comes to rest on a face that is painted white or on a face that is painted black; these two alternatives correspond to head and tail. Assuming that one does not know anything about the number or the dimensions of the black faces of the polyhedron, the probability of tail is thus unknown. The polyhedron might be a cubic die with 5 faces painted black, or it might be a wooden cube with a small piece cut off one corner and the small triangular face painted black. The following is the general problem with which we shall be concerned:

PROBLEM 49. *If $n + p$ trials have yielded n heads and p tails, what can one conclude about the probability x of getting tails?*

A priori we have no knowledge about this probability x, but we shall assume that in this state of ignorance one has the right to treat any value between 0 and 1 as equally likely. Thus, the *a priori* probability that x is contained between x_1 and x_2 equals $x_2 - x_1$, and the probability that it is contained between z and $z + dz$ equals dz. When x has the value z, the probability of getting n heads and p tails is given by

$$(1) \qquad \frac{(n + p)!}{n!p!} z^p (1 - z)^n$$

since the probability for tails is z and the probability for heads is $1 - z$. Preserving the notation of Section 12.2, the numbers w_k (the *a priori* probabilities) are equal to dz, and the numbers p_k are given by expression (1). Applying the formula of Bayes, namely,

$$P = \frac{p_k w_k}{\sum p_k w_k}$$

we cancel the factor independent of z which is common to all of the p_k, and we obtain

$$P = \frac{z^p (1 - z)^n \, dz}{\displaystyle\int_0^1 z^p (1 - z)^n \, dz}$$

This is the *a posteriori* probability for x to be contained between z and $z + dz$, namely, the probability after the observations have been made. No matter what assumption one makes about x, the probability P is an infinitesimal of the same order as dz. In other words, the probability for any particular value of x is infinitesimally small, and we will have to consider a finite interval, so that the probability that x is contained in the interval is, itself, finite.

14.2 Special Cases

PROBLEM 50. *If in the game defined in the preceding section two trials yielded two tails, what odds should one give that this result is due to the fact that for the given polyhedron the probability of getting tails exceeds 1/2?*

Substituting $p = 2$ and $n = 0$ into the formula for P, we obtain the preliminary result that

$$P = \frac{z^2 \, dz}{\displaystyle\int_0^1 z^2 \, dz} = 3z^2 \, dz$$

To obtain the probability that x exceeds 1/2, we have only to integrate between 1/2 and 1, and this gives

$$\int_{1/2}^1 3z^2 \, dz = \frac{7}{8}$$

Thus, the probability that for the given polyhedron the probability of getting tails exceeds 1/2 is 7/8, and the appropriate odds are 7 to 1.

PROBLEM 51. *If n and p are large in Problem 49 and one lets $t = \dfrac{p}{n + p}$, what is the probability that x is contained between $t - y$ and $t + y$, where y is very small?*

It should be noted that the given value of t maximizes the product $z^p(1 - z)^n$ and, hence, the element of probability P on page 141. This result is obtained by equating to zero the logarithmic derivative of the product; that is, one gets

$$\frac{p}{z} - \frac{n}{1 - z} = 0$$

and, hence,

$$\frac{z}{p} = \frac{1 - z}{n} = \frac{1}{n + p}$$

In order to evaluate the integral

$$J_{p,n} = \int_0^1 z^p(1 - z)^n \, dz$$

we use the formula

$$\frac{d}{dz}[z^{p+1}(1 - z)^n] = (p + 1)z^p(1 - z)^n - nz^{p+1}(1 - z)^{n-1}$$

which, integrated between 0 and 1, gives

$$0 = (p + 1)J_{p,n} - nJ_{p+1,n-1}$$

since the integral of the left-hand member is zero when $p + 1$ and n are positive. This last result can also be written as

$$J_{p,n} = \frac{n}{p + 1} J_{p+1,n-1}$$

and it follows that

$$J_{p,n} = \frac{n}{p + 1} \cdot \frac{n - 1}{p + 2} \cdot \frac{n - 2}{p + 3} \cdot \cdots \cdot \frac{2}{n + p - 1} \cdot \frac{1}{n + p} J_{n+p,0}$$

Since

$$J_{n+p,0} = \int_0^1 z^{n+p} \, dz = \frac{1}{n + p + 1}$$

one finally obtains

$$J_{p,n} = \frac{n!p!}{(n + p + 1)!}$$

and the element of probability P can be written as

(1) $$P = z^p(1 - z)^n \cdot \frac{(n + p + 1)!}{n!p!} \, dz$$

If we now let $z = t + y$, where y is very small, we can easily obtain the value approached by $\log P$ by means of calculations analogous to those of Section 5.1. Omitting all detail, let us merely indicate the result; letting

(2) $$y(n + p)\sqrt{\frac{n + p}{np}} = \lambda$$

we get, as a first approximation, the following value of P:

$$(3) \qquad\qquad P = \frac{1}{\sqrt{\pi}} e^{-\lambda^2} d\lambda$$

This is the formula of Laplace-Gauss, with the unit deviation defined by (2). The required probability is thus given by $\theta(\lambda)$, with λ determined by y in accordance with relation (2).

No matter how small y might be, the value of λ defined by (2) increases when n and p are increased in such a way that their ratio remains unchanged. Hence, the probability that x is contained between $t - y$ and $t + y$ approaches unity. It follows that if the number of trials is very large, one can (as would seem reasonable) consider the result as furnishing a very precise indication of the unknown probability.

Let us give a numerical example, remembering, of course, that the preceding results are based on the assumption of equal prior probabilities. Suppose one has

$$p = 800 \qquad \text{and} \qquad n = 100$$

For these values formula (2) yields $\lambda = 67.5y$ and, letting $y = 0.04$, it can be seen that the value of $\theta(2.7)$ differs from unity by a little more than 0.0001; in fact, it equals $0.99986\ldots$. Moreover, $\dfrac{p}{n+p} = \dfrac{8}{9} = 0.888\ldots$, and one can conclude with a probability of at least 0.99986 that the probability of tails is contained between 0.849 and 0.929.

Had we used the values $p = 80{,}000$ and $n = 10{,}000$, we would have obtained $\lambda = 675y$ and hence, putting $y = 0.004$ (which is ten times smaller than before), we would have arrived at the same value of $\theta(\lambda)$. It follows that the probability for tails is now contained between 0.885 and 0.893, and it can be seen that by increasing the number of trials one narrows the limits. It follows from the preceding calculations that the difference between the limits is inversely proportional to the square of the number of trials. If one defines *precision* as inversely proportional to the difference between such limits, one can say that *the precision is proportional to the square root of the number of trials* (see Section 10.5).

14.3 The True Value of a Measured Quantity

When one has observed various measurements of one and the same quantity, the problem of determining its actual value is a problem of the probability of causes, since the actual value is evidently the principal cause which determines the values of the measurements. Given a certain measurement, we could use the results of Chapter 10 and evaluate the probability of obtaining that measurement, assuming that the quantity being measured has some arbitrary value. We could then obtain the *a posteriori* probability, that is, a probability distribution, for the quantity being measured, provided the *a priori* probability is known. If one assumes uniform *a priori* probabilities, simple calculations lead again to the rule of the arithmetic mean, so that the probability that the true value differs from the mean of the observations by a given amount follows the law of Laplace. Having indicated its theoretical interest, we shall not dwell upon this point of view. So far as applications are concerned, nothing new is added to the results of Chapter 10.

CHAPTER FIFTEEN

The Determination of Causes

15.1 *Case Where the Cause is Unknown*

Problems concerning the probability of causes are frequently posed in the following form: *Is this result due to chance, or does it have a cause?* It has frequently been observed that this statement lacks precision; Bertrand insisted on this a great deal, and we shall have occasion to cite some of his observations. However, no matter how strongly one might object from a logical point of view, this does not prevent the preceding question from arising in many situations. Thus, the theory of probability cannot refuse to examine it and try to give an answer. The precision of such an answer will, of course, be limited by the lack of precision of the question, but to refuse a reply under the pretext that such a reply cannot be absolutely precise would be to place oneself in a purely abstract domain and disregard the inherent nature of applied mathematics. To be sure, mathematics can furnish precise answers to precise questions, but *practically speaking* there are hardly ever any precise questions. Those given experimentally will necessarily entail a gamble, and it follows that the same imprecision affects the resulting calculations. The so-called absolute theoretical precision of such calculations is merely an illusion.

As examples of questions in which the cause is unknown and the problem is to determine whether there is a cause one can cite extensive research in experimental psychology. For example, having observed the coincidence of physical and psychological peculiarities in a certain group of individuals, one might ask within what limits one can conclude that there really is a correlation.

Let us also point to the numerous questions one might ask concerning an author's language and style. Each writer has special habits concerning the length of words and phrases, which can easily be analyzed numerically. Such matters can be studied by means of interpolations from the texts, but questions of metric can also be phrased in statistical terms and solved with statistical techniques.

The methods of the theory of probability have also been applied to questions of art. For instance, various schools of sculpture may be characterized by the sizes of certain ratios among the parts of the human body, and numerical deviations from such ratios may make it possible to differentiate between the different schools.

In all these questions the role of mathematics is mainly that of furnishing the assumptions which must be made in order to subject the problem posed to an appropriate analysis. In spite of their interest, we shall leave these questions and others aside, and limit ourselves to certain details concerning applications that are more truly scientific; that is, we shall limit ourselves to those sciences which have been considered as such for a long time.

15.2 *The Distribution of Stars on the Celestial Sphere*

This is one of the most important questions of natural philosophy, as it touches upon the origin and the destiny of our universe. Except for some special cases, we shall ignore the distances between the stars, and this presents the first difficulty: If two or more stars are drawing together in the sky, can one conclude that they are also drawing closer together in space? There is no question here of giving a rigorous answer, but the study of probability can, in certain cases, give a very strong indication in favor of the affirmative. Unless one allows for regular arrangements analogous to those found in crystal structure (that is, arrangements whose existence one has no reason to suspect), it is clear that if two or more stars are extremely distant in space, the probabilities that their positions on the celestial sphere are approaching one another can be calculated in accordance with the principles of Section 8.6. Then if one counts only stars of a certain size, for example those visible to the naked eye or with a telescope, one could calculate the probability that a given number of stars are situated inside a small circle on the celestial sphere. If there actually are groupings for which the probability thus calculated is very small, we would be justified in thinking that the grouping has a cause other than chance, namely, that the grouping consists of stars that are actually approaching each other in space.

Although they do not seem convincing, Bertrand has raised the following objections to this way of thinking: *The Pleiades* [he said] *seem to be closer to one another than would be natural. This assertion is worthy of interest, but if one wants to translate the consequence into figures, one runs into difficulties. In order to make this " drawing closer" precise, must one look for the smallest circle containing the group? The greatest angular distance? The sum of the squares of all the distances? The area of the spherical polygon whose vertices are some of these stars while the others are in its interior? So far as the Pleiades group is concerned, these quantities are all much smaller than should be expected, so which one gives the appropriate measure of unlikelihood? If three of the stars happened to form an equilateral triangle, must one include this (which surely has a very small a priori probability) among the circumstances revealing a cause?*

What has to be translated into figures is the probability that a grouping is random and, no matter what Bertrand might say, the result will depend only to a slight degree on the particular form given to the definition of a grouping: a very small circle containing the stars, a spherical convex polygon and so forth. Practically speaking, it would seem reasonable to choose the definition which leads to the simplest calculations. Such calculations would lead to a result such as the following: Chance might yield such a grouping about once in 23,000. The moment this result has been stated, the theory of probability has done all it can and it must give way to *induction* and to the hypothesis one ultimately tries to verify (if possible) by other means.

Let us also say a word about Bertrand's idea concerning the possibility that an equilateral triangle might be formed by three stars; it reduces to a question of rounding numbers. If one considers a number selected at random from between 1,000,000 and 2,000,000, the probability that it equals 1,342,517 is one in a million, and the probability that it equals 1,500,000 is also one in a million. Nevertheless one would probably be inclined to regard the last one less probable than the first; this is due to the fact that one never considers a number such as 1,542,317 *individually*, but as a type of number, that is, numbers which are all similar in appearance. If one transcribed the number and changed some of the digits, one would have difficulty distinguishing, say, between 1,324,519 and 1,324,517. The reader will have to make an effort to be sure that the four numbers given in the preceding discussion are all different.

When one has observed a number such as the preceding one in the evaluation of an angle to the nearest tenth of a second, one would not think of asking for the probability that this angle is exactly 13°42′51.7″. Nevertheless, the angle must have some value, and no matter what this value might be to the nearest tenth of a second, one can only say that a particular measurement has an *a priori* probability of 1 in 10 million and, hence, that it is extremely unlikely. This is a sophism of the kind that tainted the analysis of scriptures which was popular in the nineteenth century.

The question is to know whether the same reservations apply also to the case where one of the angles of a triangle formed by three stars has an unusual value, say, where it equals 60 degrees (an angle in an equilateral triangle) or 45 degrees (half of a right angle). What one must say about this subject is that one must be very suspicious of the tendency to call something *unusual* unless it has been specified in advance; the number of circumstances which may appear unusual from various points of view is extremely large.*

The value of an angle determined by the relative position of three stars is a complicated function of the real position of the stars and the position of our solar system; the fact that such an angle equals exactly 6,666,666 tenths of seconds is no more remarkable than if it had been 1,234,567 tenths of seconds (which is another unusual number) or 2,387,256 tenths of seconds (namely, a number which *a priori* would not seem unusual).

On the other hand, the question concerning groupings in space is one of those which would be natural to ask *a priori*, and although the theory of probability does not allow one to answer it with certainty, it states precisely what conclusions one might draw from the observations. This is important, for it replaces heuristically the immediate inductions of common sense. Without doubt, we need no calculations in order to feel that the Milky Way is an exceptional set of stars, and various kinds of calculations would not add much to this impression. On the other hand, there may be cases where one is led to the result that the probability of a grouping is a third or a fourth, and here the presumption that there is a cause would be too weak to be of any interest. They would not prove anything, no more than the fact that someone who turns up a king in the game of Écarté is not necessarily a cheat. Between the two extreme cases, where the probability of a chance grouping is so small that it can be thought of as zero or where it is so large that one can conclude that there is a nonrandom element, there are many other cases, say, where the probability falls between 0.01 and 0.000001. Regardless of what Bertrand may have said, even in these intermediate cases the calculations are not without use and they may furnish valuable information.

15.3 *The Values of Atomic Weights*†

Chemists have contended for a long time that the values of atomic weights are most often whole numbers, although this fact has been questioned in the

---

* The following is a simple example: Consider a four-digit number such as 2,545, and suppose that one considers it as decomposed into the two two-digit numbers 25 and 45; now one observes that the two numbers end in the same digit 5, which is an unusual circumstance. Similarly, for 2,524 the two numbers 25 and 24 begin with the same digit 2, for 2,552 the two numbers 25 and 52 are symmetrical, for 2,550 the second number is twice the first, for 2,536 both numbers are squares, and so on. One can thus find something unusual about most numbers, and this is somewhat like a game with which one can amuse oneself looking, for example, at telephone numbers consisting of four-digit numbers, license plates on cars, numbers on railroad cars, and the like. Unless one is careful, one might thus be led to believe that unusual numbers are far more frequent than they should be in accordance with the theory of probability.

† I felt obliged to reproduce this section verbatim from my book published in 1909 (and written in 1908) so that the reader can appreciate how theoretical studies based on probabilities have caused considerable progress in the last 40 years in the knowledge of atomic numbers and atomic masses.

light of more precise measurements. In fact, the values acknowledged by the International Commission on Atomic Weights in 1909 are generally not integers.

Nevertheless, there exist some remarkable relationships; to cite an example from among those that are best known, the ratio of the atomic weights of carbon and oxygen is, except for errors of measurement, 3 to 8. It is thus natural to investigate whether the ratios between atomic weights are not too close to simple commensurable numbers to be attributed to chance. It would seem that the question posed in this precise form has not been studied with the care merited by its general interest (see footnote on page 148).

This question can be tied in with the theory of continued fractions and denumerable probabilities; as I have indicated in 1908–1909, one is thus led to develop the ratios of atomic weights taken two at a time in a continued fraction and to investigate whether the partial quotients take on various integral values more often than might be attributed to chance. Since the pairwise combinations of simple substances number in the thousands, one can fruitfully apply the theory of probability. The main difficulty in this investigation is the degree of precision with which each ratio is known; this problem would require a complete discussion of all the experiments by means of which the two atomic weights under consideration are related to one another. This would be a considerable job, but it would seem to be justified in the light of the interest attached to the problem.

So far as I can judge from my own calculations, this kind of study would probably lead to the conclusion that the atomic weights (at least those of certain groups of simple substances) differ very little from numbers having (among themselves) certain simple ratios. These numbers might be called the *real atomic weights*, and it would remain to be seen how one might interpret their physical significance and how one might account for the small differences between them and the values obtained experimentally. The existence of small residual differences between values obtained experimentally and certain real values which can be defined theoretically and which follow simple laws is frequently observed in the physical sciences. Since this was written (see footnote to page 148) physicists and chemists have found answers for the question we have posed.

15.4 *Biometrical Applications*

Recently, the name *biometrics* has been given to all research in which one analyzes measurements performed on living beings. We shall not go into the history of biometrics (which has been treated extensively in a study by Vito Volterra), and we shall merely cite the names of Quételet, who was associated with the early development of biometrics, and the names of Francis Galton and Karl Pearson.

The kinds of problems one poses in biometrics are of a great variety; in this book we shall merely indicate two of the most important ones, those dealing with the homogeneity of populations and those dealing with the subject of correlation.

Suppose one measures the waist of a great number of French adults. If one looks upon the mean of these measurements as the true value of the waist of a Frenchman, one finds that the "errors," namely, the positive and negative differences between this theoretical value and the observed values, distribute themselves in accordance with the law of Laplace. The situation appears as if all Frenchmen had exactly the same size waist, equal to the mean, and that they were being measured by a very incompetent experimenter, so that the errors of measurement follow the law of Laplace. Using the language introduced in Section 10.3, we could say that the waists of Frenchmen constitute a *normal* population. Biologically, this is in accordance with the fact that the French people constitute a sufficiently homogeneous biological group.

Suppose now that one performs the same experiment in a town where the inhabitants belong to two different races—say, some of them are caucasians and some of them are orientals. If one measured all the adult inhabitants and recorded the measurements without recording the race, one would find that the mean no longer has the same significance and that the distribution of the values about the mean is not as simple as the one given by the law of Laplace. One obtains the superposition of two distinct phenomena, each following the law of Laplace, which together do not follow this law. The waists of the first subpopulation are grouped about their mean in accordance with the law of Laplace, and those of the second subpopulation are similarly distributed about their mean. The over-all mean has no real significance; it may very well be that it does not even represent the value having the highest frequency. This expresses the biological fact that there are two distinct subpopulations, and had this not been known it would have been revealed by an analysis of the distribution and its mean.

Without delving deeper into this subject (to which one could devote a whole book), it should be noted that the experimental study of analogous phenomena leads to the following general conclusion: *The biometric characteristic intrinsic to normal series is the purity of the corresponding populations.* We shall not go into the detailed discussion that would be required to justify such a general statement; it is up to the biologist rather than the mathematician to make these ideas more precise. Be this as it may, the theory has proven to be of great scientific value and useful in many practical applications. Let us mention just one instance, the interesting work done in Sweden with different varieties of barley. Applying the statistical concept of the purity of populations they obtained an extremely pure strain of barley, whose constancy was very much appreciated by the brewers by whom the scientists were employed. In a situation like this the question of homogeneity is of great industrial importance.

The theory of correlation is equally as interesting as the biometrical theory of homogeneity, since it can provide clues in problems of heredity. If various kinds of measurements are made of individuals belonging to the same race, one is led to ask what relationships there might exist between the different kinds of measurements. For instance, knowing the size of a person's waist, can one conclude anything about the size of the forearm of his son? It can be seen how the concept of a cause is thus singularly enlarged; ordinarily one would not say that the size of a person's waist is the cause of the length of the forearm of his son. From the viewpoint of probability theory, this extension of the notion of a cause is perfectly legitimate. I am referring here mainly to the work done on the theory of correlation by Karl Pearson and his followers, published mainly in the *Proceedings of the Royal Society of London* and in *Biometrika*. I am also limiting this discussion of correlation to point to the modern methods of genetics, where the theory of probability enters whenever there is a choice between the chromosomes of a person's two parents.

15.5 *Conclusion*

The purpose of this discussion has been to demonstrate the vastness of the field of application of the theory of probability. Some of the applications were passed over very quickly, and there are many others that were not even mentioned. The theory of probability is the science of populations, and in many problems of biology and the social sciences the modern tendency is to substitute the study of populations for that of individuals. This substitution is often delicate, since the question of knowing when to consider a population as an essentially homogeneous whole is a difficult one. The theory of probability often gives valuable indications with regard to this fundamental question.

In conclusion I want to repeat a remark which I have made several times, a remark whose importance cannot be stressed too strongly: The theory of probability, like all other mathematical theories, cannot resolve *a priori* concrete questions which belong to the domain of experience. Its only role—beautiful in itself—is to guide experience and observations by the interpretation it furnishes for their results.

Appendices

Psychological Games
and the Imitation of Chance

I.1 *Extension of the Calculus of Probability to Human Problems*

It was the study of very simple games, notably games played with dice, that led to the development of the principles of the calculus of probability, and it has been in this area that the new science has made its greatest progress. Nowadays, the extent of the applicability of the theory of probability has grown considerably, and one might say that this theory plays a role in all of the natural sciences. Nevertheless, there are certain problems for which the application of the calculus of probability appears rather questionable, and where it meets difficulties which have not yet been resolved. We are referring here to problems involving an element of human psychology, notably problems of economics.

Before one approaches these complex problems in their full generality, it would seem best to begin by studying some simple cases connected with games involving an element of chance as well as the psychology of the players. This kind of situation arises in most card games, even in the simplest ones. However, before we do this, that is, before we investigate games involving chance as well as the skill of the players, we shall consider games which might be called psychological games. In such games chance has no bearing and the entire action takes place in the minds of the players.

I.2 *Definition of Psychological Games*

The simplest psychological game is the game of *even or odd*, which can assume various forms among which the following is the simplest. Each of two players A and B writes down a positive integer without knowledge of the number chosen by the other; for the sake of simplicity, one might agree that the number must be either 1 or 2. If the sum of the two numbers is *even* A wins; if it is *odd* B wins.*

It is evident that if player B always chooses an even number, A would be sure to win by also choosing an even number; of course, B would probably lose no time in discovering this strategy and choose an odd number instead. More generally, if B showed a preference for even numbers, that is, if he choose even numbers more often than odd numbers, it is easy to see that it would be to A's advantage also to show a preference for even numbers, without actually choosing them all the time so that B would not discover his strategy. We shall return to this simple game later on, but let us first consider another psychological game that is slightly more complicated.

Suppose that each player must choose one of the letters A, B, or C, and that A beats B, B beats C, and C beats A, while the game is a tie when both players choose the same letter. This game is known in the Far East in the following form: A stands for paper, B stands for stone, and C stands for scissor. (Note that the paper can be used to wrap the stone, the stone can be used to sharpen the scissors, and the scissors can be used to cut the paper.) At a given signal each player indicates paper by extending his right hand with the fingers flat, stone by making a fist, and scissors by showing the middle and index fingers while the others are closed. It is essential, of course, that the two players act simultaneously, so that each player does not know what his opponent is going to do. As in the game of *even or odd*, one must anticipate what one's opponent is going to do; to win, one must at least be able to anticipate what he will do most often.

I.3 *Application of Probabilities to Psychological Games*

Let us now assume that in a psychological game each player has a fixed probability for making each choice, and that this probability does not vary over a given period of time. In the game of even or odd, for example, we might suppose that player A chooses his moves by drawing numbered counters out of a bag; if there are m even-numbered counters and n odd-numbered counters, the probability that A will choose an even number is $p = \dfrac{m}{m + n}$, and this probability will remain constant if each counter is replaced and the counters are thoroughly mixed before the next one is drawn. If player B proceeds in the same way, he will have a probability q of choosing an even number.

---

* In some countries the game is played as follows: At a given signal each player must open his fist and show a numbers of fingers; A wins if and only if the total number of fingers extended is even.

For player A to win, it is necessary that the sum of the two numbers drawn is even, namely, that they are both even or both odd; evidently, the probability that this will happen is

$$P = pq + (1 - p)(1 - q)$$

If one lets $p = 1/2 + \alpha$ and $q = 1/2 + \beta$, where α and β are small positive or negative numbers, the expression for this probability simplifies to

$$P = (\tfrac{1}{2} + \alpha)(\tfrac{1}{2} + \beta) + (\tfrac{1}{2} - \alpha)(\tfrac{1}{2} - \beta) = \tfrac{1}{2} + 2\alpha\beta$$

It can be seen from this formula that P exceeds $1/2$, namely, that player A has an advantage, if α and β have the same sign; similarly, player B has an advantage if α and β are of opposite sign. If either α or β is equal to zero, the chances of the two players are the same. Thus, if A knows that his opponent is a better player than he, he has only to put $\alpha = 0$ in order to make the game equitable; in fact, the psychological game thus reduces to an equitable game of chance. This is evident, since no matter what B does, if A draws from a bag having as many even counters as odd counters, there is exactly one chance in two that the choice will be odd or even; in other words, there is one chance in two of making the same choice as B and, hence, one chance in two of winning.

However, if B does not choose $\beta = 0$, player A can try to win by giving α the same sign as β; at the same time he would try to hide his choice from B, which would not be the case if α were very large. Since a long series of games would divulge the sign of β, B might adopt the following rule: He would try to make A think that β is positive and then change it to negative. For example, in the first 10 games B might choose 7 even numbers and 3 odd numbers (which corresponds to $\beta = 0.2$), and then switch his preference to odd numbers. Of course, A may discover this change in tactics immediately and act accordingly. We shall not go into the various possibilities that might arise, but we shall return to this problem later in a section devoted to the imitation of chance.

I.4 *Varying Stakes*

The game described in Section I.2 may be generalized in an interesting fashion by varying the stakes. One might thus consider three positive numbers a, b, and c (say, dollars) so that

> there is a payoff of c dollars when A beats B
>
> there is a payoff of a dollars when B beats C
>
> there is a payoff of b dollars when C beats A

We shall suppose that one of the players, player J, chooses A, B, and C with the respective probabilities x, y, and z (where $x + y + z = 1$), and that the

other player, player J′ chooses A, B, and C with the respective probabilities
x', y', and z' (where $x' + y' + z' = 1$). The probability that J chooses A
while J′ chooses B is xy', and in that case J wins c dollars; the probability
that J chooses B while J′ chooses A is $x'y$, and in that case J loses c dollars.
It follows that the expected gain of player J is

$$G = (xy' - yx')c + (yz' - zy')a + (zx' - xz')b$$

which can also be written as

$$G = x(cy' - bz') + y(az' - cx') + z(bx' - ay')$$

Using the identity

$$a(cy' - bz') + b(az' - cx') + c(bx' - ay') = 0$$

we find that since a, b, and c are positive, the three quantities $cy' - bz'$,
$az' - cx'$, and $bx' - ay'$ cannot be all positive or all negative. Hence, x, y,
and z can be chosen in such a way that G is positive.

This fact can be demonstrated more instructively by writing G in the following form as a third-order determinant:

$$G = \begin{vmatrix} x & y & z \\ x' & y' & z' \\ a & b & c \end{vmatrix}$$

To give this determinant a geometrical interpretation, consider a triangle
ABC (which may be assumed to be equilateral), a point M whose distances

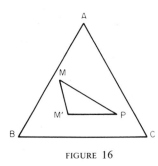

FIGURE 16

from the sides BC, CA, and AB are proportional to x, y, z, a point M' whose corresponding distances are proportional to x', y',
and z', and a point P for which these distances
are proportional to a, b, and c. These three
points are all inside the triangle since x, y, z,
x', y', z', a, b, and c are all assumed to be
positive. It is easy to see that the determinant
G is positive when the triangle $MM'P$ has the
same *disposition* as the triangle ABC, and that
otherwise it is negative. The disposition of a
triangle is the sense in which one must turn
to follow the order in which the vertices are listed. In our figure (Figure 16)
the disposition of ABC is counterclockwise, and so is the disposition of
$MM'P$. On the other hand, it is evident that ACB and MPM' have clock-
wise dispositions.

It is clear from our figure, where the two triangles have the same disposition, that one can make ABC coincide with $MM'P$ by means of a continuous
deformation throughout which the determinant G does not vanish, for

the determinant is zero only when the points M, M', and P lie on a straight line. Since the determinant varies continuously when x, y, and z vary continuously (or x', y', z', a, b, c), it preserves its sign as it does not pass through zero. When $MM'P$ coincides with ABC the determinant G reduces to

$$G_1 = \begin{vmatrix} 1 & 0 & 0 \\ 0 & 1 & 0 \\ 0 & 0 & 1 \end{vmatrix} = 1$$

and it is thus positive for the triangle $MM'P$ of Figure 16.

It follows that if x', y', z', a, b, and c are such that the points M' and P do not coincide (that is, x', y', and z' must not be proportional to a, b, and c), one has only to choose M on the appropriate side of $M'P$ to make G positive. Thus, if player J knows x', y', and z', namely, the strategy of player J', he could choose a strategy which would assure him a positive expectation, and hence a certain gain in the long run. Inversely, if player J' knows x, y, and z, namely, the strategy of player J, he could choose the point M' so that G is negative, and this would assure him a gain in the long run. To accomplish this he has only to choose M' on the appropriate side of PM.

If player J wants to make certain that J' will not win but he does not know his strategy, he has only to make M coincide with P, namely, to choose x, y, and z so that $x/a = y/b = z/c$. In that case G is zero and the game is equitable no matter what player J' might choose to do.

I.5 *An Example*

Suppose that J and J' each have a large number of playing cards which are either spades, hearts, or diamonds, and that they are playing under the following rules:

> spades beats hearts and wins   100 dollars
>
> hearts beats diamonds and wins   10 dollars
>
> diamonds beats spades and wins   1 dollar

We shall also suppose that J has x spades, y hearts, and z diamonds, and that he plays by randomly selecting one card, replacing it, and shuffling before the next one is drawn. Using the result obtained in the preceding section, let us put $c = 100$, $a = 10$, and $b = 1$, so that $x/10 = y/1 = z/100$. To make the game equitable, he must thus have 10 spades, 1 heart, and 100 diamonds. It is remarkable that the suit which yields the smallest gain has the largest number. Hearts must be least because they can lead to the greatest loss. One might ask whether it might not be preferable to leave out the one heart altogether, thus eliminating the possibility of losing 100 dollars. It is evident, however, that if player J has only two suits, spades and diamonds for example, player J′ cannot possibly lose by always playing the one of these two colors which beats the other (in our case diamonds, since diamonds beats spades).

On the other hand, if J′ always played spades in 111 games he would on the average win 100 dollars from hearts once and lose 1 dollar to diamonds 100 times; if J′ always played hearts in 111 games he would on the average lose 100 dollars to spades 10 times and win 10 dollars from diamonds 100 times. Finally, if J′ always played diamonds in 111 games he would on the average win 1 dollar from spades 100 times and lose 100 dollars to spades once. The game is thus equitable in each case and, hence, also for any arbitrary strategy of player J′.

I.6 *The Imitation of Chance*

In the preceding example we have shown how player J can conform to the rules by randomly drawing a card from a hand having a certain composition. One might thus ask whether it is actually necessary to make such a random drawing and whether there might not be some other means by which he could proceed and still be certain that his opponent cannot take advantage of him from observing his method of play. The problem we have posed is none other than that of the imitation of chance: *Is it possible for the human mind to imitate chance?* Limiting ourselves to the simplest case, the game of even or odd, can a person choosing numbers (even or odd) indefinitely be so clever that the sequence he chooses cannot be distinguished from one selected by chance?

To be able to answer this question, we shall first have to formulate it more precisely, that is, we shall have to try to determine the characteristics by which one can tell whether a given sequence was obtained by chance, or at least *whether it may be regarded as having been obtained by chance.* This question may seem insolvable since chance can lead to any sequence whatsoever and, rigorously speaking, even the most improbable is not impossible. Speaking in an absolute sense, it is not impossible to obtain 1,000 heads in a row in *heads or tails*, or 1,000 even numbers in a row in *even or odd*, but the probability of such a result is $2^{-1,000}$, or approximately 10^{-300}, and it is so improbable that it may be regarded as impossible. Thus, the problem should be restated as follows: We must consider a sequence as possibly having been obtained by chance if it does not present certain general characteristics which are highly improbable in a random sequence.

The simplest of these characteristics is the proportion in which the two alternatives (heads or tail, even or odd) occur. On the average, each alternative should be obtained the same number of times, for instance, 500 times in 1,000 trials. More precisely, a deviation of $\sqrt{500}$, or approximately 22, has a small probability, but it will nevertheless be observed fairly often in a great number of experiments. On the other hand, a deviation twice as large, that is, a deviation of 44, is already very improbable, and a deviation of 88 has a probability which is so small that if such a deviation is observed one can say that the sequence does not present one of the characteristics essential for a random sequence. We shall thus discard as nonrandom sequences of 1,000 experiments in which one of the alternatives occurs more than 600 or fewer than 400 times.

I.7 *The Study of Runs*

It would be relatively easy for a player to imitate chance if he had only to satisfy the preceding condition, that is, if he had only to choose the two alternatives with the same frequency. Actually, this is far from being enough, as is illustrated by the following: One has only to picture a naive player who alternately selects even and odd in order to make sure that the alternatives appear equally often. It is clear, without even performing any calculations, that the resulting sequence is very special and that it cannot be considered as having been obtained by chance.

In order to study the problem in more detail, let us briefly investigate what one refers to as *runs* in a series of heads or tails. A run is a series of identical results, for example, heads, which is preceded and followed by a result of a different kind. We use this term even in the case where a run consists of but one element; for example, the sequence

TTTHTHHTTTHHHHTHTTHHTHHHHHTTT

where H stands for heads and T for tails, consists of a run of 3 tails, a run of 1 head, a run of 1 tail, a run of 2 heads, a run of 3 tails, a run of 4 heads, a run of 1 tail, a run of 1 head, a run of 2 tails, a run of 2 heads, a run of 1 tail, a run of 5 heads, and a run of 3 tails. Thus, there are 5 runs of length 1, 2 runs of length 2, 3 runs of length 3, 1 run of length 4, and 1 run of length 5.

It can easily be shown that in a series of n trials there are on the average $n/4$ runs of length 1, of which $n/8$ are runs of heads and $n/8$ are runs of tails. The average number of runs of length 2 is half of $n/4$, or $n/8$, and the average number of runs of length 3 is half of $n/8$, or $n/16$, and so on.

In a series of 1,000 trials one should thus obtain on the average 250 runs of length 1. Note that a player who alternately selects heads and tails will get 1,000 runs of length 1, and without going into any detail let us merely state that a series of 1,000 trials in which there are more than 300 or fewer than 200 runs of length 1 does not present one of the characteristics essential for a random sequence.

It has been observed that some players, selecting between even and odd, have a tendency to produce too many runs of length 1, apparently to make sure of the balance between the number of evens and the number of odds. On the other hand, other players have a tendency to select too many long runs, think that this will prevent their opponents from taking advantage of them by anticipating changes from even to odd (or odd to even).

In a series of 1,000 trials there are on the average 250 runs of length 1, but this is not all; these runs may be isolated or they may appear in groups. It is easy to see that on the average one-fourth, or about 62 of the runs, should be isolated (that is, neither preceded nor followed by another run of length 1). Also there should be on the average half of 62, or 31, pairs of adjacent runs of length 1, there should be on the average half of 31, or about 16, sequences of three consecutive runs of length 1, and so forth. These numbers become too small to base judgements on their deviations, but one should discard as nonrandom any series of 1,000 trials in which there is not at least one sequence of 4 consecutive runs of length 1.

The 250 runs of length 1 which one can expect in 1,000 trials can also be studied from a different point of view. Considering the order in which they were obtained they constitute a new sequence of H's and T's, and this new sequence of 250 letters must have the same general characteristics as the whole sequence of 1,000 letters. For instance, there must be about 62 runs of length 1 among the 250 H's and T's.

It is easy to indicate further conditions which must be satisfied by runs of length 1 and their groupings, but this will rapidly lead to a great number of conditions which must be satisfied if one wants to imitate chance, that is, if one wants to construct *mentally* a sequence of 1,000 H's and T's which has some of the characteristics that are essential for drawings of this kind. There can be no doubt that it would actually be simpler to resort to random drawings, since this would enable one to satisfy all the conditions mentioned as well as many others. Of course, this criterion of simplicity does not completely resolve the problem, and we must still ask whether a mathematician (who has studied the problem thoroughly) might not arrive at a method which he could use to imitate chance.

I.8 *The Impossiblity of Imitating Chance*

We shall now demonstrate that such an imitation is impossible, and to this end we shall assume that we have actually found a rule which enables us to make a random choice of even or odd, which takes into account everything that happened in all preceding trials (that is, the choice made by both players).

Indeed, if we did not account for what happened in the preceding trials, this would mean that our method of choice is the same for each trial; in other words, our probability for choosing between even and odd would have to be constant (and, hence, equal to 1/2 since we would otherwise not be imitating chance). This being so, we must admit that someone who carefully watches our manner of play would (if he is as intelligent as we are) discover the rules which control our play.

This is precisely what amateurs at roulette try to do; they hope to discover a law controlling successive results, but they fail because a roulette wheel does not obey any laws except those of chance. The situation would be different if an intelligent player accounted for all previous plays, sometimes choosing even in preference to odd (or vice versa) in accordance with the observations he has made in the preceding trials, especially with reference to the nature, the number, and the arrangement of runs. However, the moment an intelligent opponent discovers the law that is used to imitate chance, he could adjust his play accordingly and, thus, assure himself of a definite advantage. The player who wants to imitate chance is thus at a disadvantage, and this would not have happened if he actually made physical or mental drawings to determine his play.*

I.9 *Application to Parlor Games*

In most card games which are called parlor games (bridge, poker, etc.), the interest in the game arises from the fact that it depends on chance as well as on the competence of the players. It is easy to see, however, that in most of these games a player who follows immutable rules, that is, a player who always plays the same way under the same conditions would find himself at a disadvantage; his opponent might discover his mode of play and modify his strategy accordingly.

These games are too complicated to develop for them a complete mathematical theory (which moreover would remove a good deal of their interest), but it should be noted that such a theory would have to lead to fixed probabilities, that is, it would have to indicate for each situation how a player must choose between two or more alternatives with fixed probabilities.

In fact, if a poker player always played the same way in a given situation, his opponents would be able to deduce information from his mode of play (without much chance of being deceived), and they could use this information to their advantage. Consequently, if one could establish a mathematical theory for correctly playing poker (which actually is too complicated a problem to be solved completely), the rules of such a theory would ultimately have to be formulated in terms of probabilities such as the following, pertaining to a situation which might arise during the course of play: After his opponents have made certain known moves, a player with a given hand must drop out with the probability p', pass with the probability p'', or raise an amount $r_1, r_2, \ldots$, or r_n with respective probability of $p_1, p_2, \ldots$, or p_n. Some of these probabilities may be zero, but their sum must always equal 1. Since a player cannot very well interrupt a game to make random drawings, he will have to be satisfied with mental drawings (see footnote), in which he

---

* If one does not have at one's disposal material objects to perform random drawings, one might think of words or phrases, count the letters, and thus choose between even and odd. This might be referred to as making mental drawings.

imitates chance as much as possible, without giving himself away by hesi-
tating before making his move. In actual practice, it is always preferable
to make random drawings (perhaps, by lot) than to be guided by mental
drawings which might be affected by the results of previous ones. For
example, if the rule says that one should bluff with a probability of 1/6,
random drawings might nevertheless lead to two consecutive bluffs. Thus,
the opponent who knows that the previous occasion was a bluff does not
know whether this time it is again a bluff or a good play.

I.10 *Intelligence, Intuition, and the Imitation of Chance*

We have seen that the human intelligence is incapable of imitating chance,
and it suggests itself that this might be the reason why some people (under
certain conditions) rely on their intuition to win over those who rely on
their intelligence. The examples we have given all pertained to games, but
we could just as well have given examples relating, say, to problems of
military strategy or economics. Suppose one has to defend three points
against an agressor whose total forces are identical with those of the
defense; the problem might involve 10 policemen and 10 crooks, or a fight
between 10 armies (navies, or air forces) and 10 other armies (navies, or
air forces).

It is evident that he who knows the disposition of his opponent's forces
can assure himself an advantage at two of the three points. For example,
the disposition 4, 3, 3 wins at two points over 6, 2, 2, since $4 < 6$, $3 > 2$,
and $3 > 2$. Similarly, 6, 2, 2 wins at two points over 5, 4, 1, which in turn
wins at two points over 4, 3, 3. An analogous situation might face two
merchants, where each is willing to sacrifice a certain sum by reducing the
prices of certain products in order to lure away some of his competitor's
customers.

In all these examples it was assumed that each of the opposing players
must plan his strategy in secret and that he cannot modify it suddenly after
he learns something about the strategy chosen by his opponent. Being
ignorant of one's opponent's plans, a sure way not to be taken advantage
of is to rely on chance. This will prevent one's opponent from using his
intelligence to guess one's intention and thus put one at a disadvantage,
since the human intelligence is incapable of imitating chance. One might
thus ask whether a certain person's superiority of play might not be due to
the fact that he possesses an intuition which enables him to imitate chance
unconsciously (that is, make a mental drawing) where intelligence fails.

APPENDIX TWO

Objective and Subjective Probabilities

II.1 *Are There Objective Probabilities?*

Henri Poincaré repeatedly insisted on making a distinction between objective and subjective probabilities; in contrast, John Maynard Keynes, in his *Treatise of Probability*, maintained that all probabilities are subjective. What are their reasons? The answer to this question is up against the popular opinion that the British are generally more practical and concrete, while the French are generally more theoretical and abstract. In fact, we shall see that whereas Keynes reasons from an abstract point of view, Poincaré's opinions are justified on practical grounds.

There can be no doubt that probabilities, as they are known to us, are creations of the human mind. An omniscient being who knows all the mechanisms of the universe in all details would need no probabilities.* Probabilities exist in the human mind and they depend on, and are determined by, the body of knowledge K contained in that mind. This body of knowledge is not always exactly the same for two different minds, nor is it always the same even for one and the same mind at two different times. Thus, one should never speak of the probability of an event (say, a particular outcome of a roll of a pair of dice), but of the probability for Peter who rolls the dice, or for Paul who observes the throw, perhaps after having placed a bet. Denoting the event by a and Peter or Paul's body of knowledge by K, we denote the corresponding probability by $P(a, K)$.

---

* We shall leave aside all considerations concerning the modern theories of wave mechanics, according to which certain real phenomena can be defined only in terms of probabilities.

Although Poincaré did not systematically use this notation of Keynes (or an analogous notation), he did not ignore the fact that the probability of an event can be different for two observers who do not have the same information concerning the circumstances surrounding the event. This is precisely what he meant when he said that certain probabilities are subjective, namely, that their values are exact only for a certain person. Nevertheless, he maintained that there are certain probabilities which have the same value for a great many people, since the body of knowledge referred to as K by Keynes is practically the same for each. These are the probabilities which Poincaré called objective and this terminology is correct, clear, and appropriate, even though it might be contested by a metaphysician in whose eyes no human knowledge can be called objective.

Considering the roll of a pair of dice, for instance, if the onlookers know that the dice are properly fabricated and that they are rolled with sufficient force so that they do not immediately come to rest, the probability of each face is the same, equal to $1/6$, and it is an objective probability.

The situation is the same if one considers the probability of being dealt a given hand in a card game (say, bridge or poker), provided the cards are thoroughly shuffled and dealt by an honest player. For all players or spectators, the body of knowledge K is the same; they all know the composition of the deck and the fact that the person who deals the cards is not dishonest. Thus, we conclude with Poincaré that it is legitimate to speak of objective probabilities in certain situations, but this will not stop us from using the notation of Keynes to study subjective probabilities.

II.2 *The Probability of Death*

Among the objective probabilities cited by Poincaré are those used by insurance companies in establishing their rates. The regularity with which these companies pay dividends to their stockholders supports the objectivity of their calculations. This is a particularly interesting example, since probabilities concerning human life may be regarded as objective or subjective, depending on one's point of view.

Insurance companies use mortality tables, prepared in accordance with precise rules which we shall not discuss. It is to these mortality tables that they attribute an objective value on the grounds of experience.

Nevertheless, insurance companies take precautions to prevent the assured from modifying the odds by introducing subjective elements into the considerations. In fact, it is evident that if a man knows that he has a serious (perhaps fatal) disease, he would be interested in insuring his life to benefit his heirs. Thus, if the insurance company did not insist that the assured take a medical examination before the policy is signed, the mortality rates of persons with insurance would be much higher than the rates given in the table.

It is for the same reason that insurance companies refuse to insure the risk of suicide, at least, not for a certain number of years after the policy is signed. The case where a person contemplates suicide is, in fact, a typical case of subjective probability. His probability of dying is much higher than it would be for someone lucky enough to be in good health. For those planning suicide, the probability would have to be based on special statistics concerning suicide rates.

Once the necessary precautions have been taken, the probabilities used by the insurance companies are objective with the following reservation: They must be considered as universal and not as individual probabilities. It is evident that among 1,000 men insured at age 30 after a medical examination who have reached the age of 60, the probabilities of dying can vary considerably. Some of them will be in good health while others will be seriously ill. So far as the insurance company's actuary is concerned, he does not make this distinction. The body of knowledge K consists merely of the fact that the insured passed a medical examination at age 30 and has reached age 60. This enables him to calculate the probability $P(a, K)$ that a of the 1,000 men will die during the next year. On the other hand, their probabilities of dying within a year would vary greatly in the eyes of a competent doctor who has given them careful examinations; they would be much higher than average for some individuals and lower for others.

II.3 *The Probability of an Isolated Case*

Some theorists in the field of probability would criticize the language we have used, claiming that one cannot speak of the probability of an isolated event; they feel that all applied probabilities must reduce to statements concerning relative frequencies. This is the theory of the *collective* which has been analyzed and refuted with great skill by J. Ville. Without going into this problem in any detail, let us merely indicate how one can evaluate at least approximately the probability of an isolated case by referring to betting.

To illustrate, let us consider a match between two tennis players who have never played against one another; however, each of them has played in many tournaments and an enlightened amateur can appreciate the quality of their play. Suppose now that we ask such an amateur to evaluate the probability that one of the two players will win the match. It is assumed that the match is of sufficient importance so that each player will make a maximum effort to win.

If the amateur does not recognize probabilities referring to isolated events, he might refuse to evaluate this probability, since it refers to an event which (so far as we are concerned) cannot be reproduced a second time. To force him to give us an evaluation we might resort to methods based on betting. One cannot force a person to bet, that is, risk part of his fortune, but few persons would refuse to accept a present offered in exchange for a small intellectual effort. We thus make the amateur the following proposition: We offer him a certain amount which he can win in two different ways, either by rolling at least 10 with three dice or by betting on player A. If he chooses the second alternative, that is, he prefers to bet on player A, we can conclude that he regards the probability of this event as greater than that of betting on the dice, namely, greater than 0.50. Then we could ask him to choose between betting on player A or betting on getting 1, 2, 3, or 4 with a single die. If he chooses the last alternative, which has a probability of 2/3, we can conclude that he considers the probability of player A winning as being less than 2/3. We have thus obtained two limits, 0.50 and 0.67, containing the probability p that player A will win. It would be possible to obtain more stringent limits by analogous means, so that the result would be exact to at least one decimal; for example we might find that the probability is contained between 0.50 and 0.60. It might seem that this result is rather crude, but it often happens in the natural sciences that certain experimental constants are known only very crudely, and such approximate knowledge certainly differs from total ignorance.

One might compare the empirical evaluation of the probability of an isolated case with an assessment an architect or contractor might make of the dimensions of a building without actually using any measuring instruments. Such an assessment would obviously be less precise than a measurement with a yardstick, which in turn would be less precise than a measurement a physicist might make with more perfect measuring instruments. In spite of this, one might observe that in an absolute sense there really is no great difference in knowing a number between 0 and 1 correct to one decimal, two decimals, . . . , or seven decimals.

No matter what kinds of measurements are used, one can always diminish the error to a considerable extent by repeating the measurements several times (either by the same person or by different persons) and then using the average of the results obtained. One might proceed in the same way in the evaluation of probabilities. Returning to the example of the two tennis players, one might consult several amateurs about the probability that one of the players will win and then take the average of their evaluations. If the number of amateurs consulted is sufficiently large, it would be reasonable to look upon the probability thus obtained as an objective probability. We shall return to this question in Section II.5, which is devoted to pari-mutuel betting.

II.4 Individual Probabilities of Death

Let us now say a word about an individual person's probability of dying, looking upon this probability as that of an isolated event. Statistical observations provide us with probabilities for the inhabitants of a country or a large town, taking into account only a person's sex and his matrimonial status (single, married, widowed, or divorced*). In spite of the shortcomings of certain statistics, one knows the probabilities of dying at a given age from various diseases and from various kinds of accidents.

If one wants to know the probability that a man will survive for at least one year with the greatest possible precision, one would have to examine one by one the possible causes of death and attempt to evaluate for him the corresponding probabilities. So far as diseases are concerned, one must account for the development of new medicines, and one must recognize the fact that there is a nonnegligible probability that a contagious disease might spread rapidly in the course of a year and affect a person otherwise in excellent health. So far as deaths resulting from accidents are concerned, it would be useful to know something about a person's profession and his activities. One could thus obtain a universal probability which applies to the individual, even though no two human beings of the same age are exactly alike so far as their activities and their medical records are concerned.

Moreover, it is evident that if one considers the probability that a man of 40 will die between the ages of 70 and 71, this probability would be greatly affected by everything one can learn *today* about the individual, making it approach the above-mentioned universal probability given by the statistician. One might also observe that if the man in question contracts an incurable disease at age 40, the probability that he will die between the ages of 70 and 71 is practically zero, as it is almost certain that he will die before reaching that age. On the other hand, the probability of dying between the ages of 70 and 71 can be much less than the statistical probability for someone aged 40, if at that age he is in excellent health.

II.5 *Pari-Mutuel Betting*

Let us now turn to an entirely different subject, namely, to pari-mutuel betting as it is practiced at the race track; actually, it applies just as well to other competitive sports, elections, and so forth. This is a particularly interesting subject inasmuch as it involves the probability of an isolated case as well as the distinction between objective and subjective probabilities.

To simplify the problem, we shall ignore the deduction of a certain percentage to defray administrative costs and taxes. We might thus picture a small group of friends who (among themselves) have arranged some sort of private pari-mutuel betting scheme.

The following is the basic problem faced by a bettor A: Knowing the total amounts bet on the various eventualities, should he bet on a given event E, and if so, how much? We shall simplify the problem without loss

---

* A bachelor's probability of dying is greater than that of a married man, and the reason may be that the latter generally lives in a healthier environment. On the other hand, bachelors in poor health are more apt to remain unmarried, and this may be why a bachelor's probability of dying is greater.

of generality by combining all the other eventualities and referring to them as E'. The respective probabilities for E and E' are p and p' (where $p + p' = 1$), and the respective sums already bet on E and E' are s and s'. Let us now determine the mathematical expectation of a player A who bets the additional amount a on E, so that the total amount bet on E is $s + a$. Thus, if E occurred player A would win

$$g = \frac{as'}{s + a}$$

and if E' occurred his losses would equal a. Since the corresponding probabilities are p and p', the mathematical expectation $\varphi(a)$ is given by

(1) $$\varphi(a) = \frac{as'p}{s + a} - p'a$$

This function vanishes at $a = 0$ and at a_0, where a is given by

(2) $$a_0 = \frac{ps' - p's}{p'}$$

It can easily be seen that the function $\varphi(a)$ is positive for all values of a between 0 and a_0; thus, for the mathematical expectation to be positive it is necessary that a_0 be positive, namely, that

(3) $$ps' - p's > 0$$

Assuming that this condition is satisfied, let us now determine the maximum value of $\varphi(a)$. This value is obtained by equating to zero the derivative of $\varphi(a)$ with respect to a; we thus get

$$\varphi'(a) = \frac{pss'}{(s + a)^2} - p'$$

This gives

(4) $$(s + a)^2 = \frac{pss'}{p'} = s^2 + s \cdot \frac{ps' - p's}{p'} = s^2 + sa_0$$

which can also be written as

(5) $$(s + a)^2 = \left(s + \frac{a_0}{2}\right)^2 - \frac{a_0^2}{4}$$

If we assume that a_0 is small compared to s, we find that a equals approximately $a_0/2$. More rigorously, we have

$$s + a = s\sqrt{1 + \frac{a_0}{s}} = s\left(1 + \frac{a_0}{2s} - \frac{1}{8} \cdot \frac{a_0^2}{s^2} + \ldots\right)$$

or

$$a = \frac{a_0}{2} - \frac{1}{8} \cdot \frac{a_0^2}{s} + \ldots = \frac{a_0}{2}\left(1 - \frac{1}{4} \cdot \frac{a_0}{s} + \ldots\right)$$

Observing that (3) can be written in the form

(6)
$$\frac{s}{p} < \frac{s'}{p'}$$

and that the fraction $\dfrac{s + s'}{p + p'} = s + s'$ assumes a value between s/p and s'/p',

it follows from (6) that

(7)
$$\frac{s}{p} < s + s'$$

We can now state the following rule: If there are n possible events $E_1, E_2, \ldots,$ E_n, and their respective probabilities are $p_1, p_2, \ldots, p_n$, we are assured a positive mathematical expectation by betting a suitable sum on any one of the event E_i for which

(8)
$$\frac{s_i}{p_i} < s_1 + s_2 + \ldots + s_n$$

where $s_1, s_2, \ldots, s_n$ are the total amounts already bet on $E_1, E_2, \ldots,$ and E_n. There will always be events E_i satisfying this condition unless

(9)
$$\frac{s_1}{p_1} = \frac{s_2}{p_2} = \ldots = \frac{s_n}{p_n}$$

in which case the mathematical expectation of each original bettor is zero and the game is equitable. Note that the mathematical expectation will then be negative for any additional bettor who bets, without there being a counter bet, on any one of the events.

II.6 Pari-Mutuel Betting and Subjective Probabilities

In the preceding section we based our argument on the assumption that the probabilities p_i were well determined and that they were the same for each bettor. In practice, this is seldom the case, since each bettor personally interprets the information he has (or believes to have), and such information is generally not the same for all bettors. As a result, relation (8) is generally satisfied for all values of i from 1 to n, but of course for different bettors whose subjective estimates of the corresponding probabilities p_i are greater than those of the other bettors. It thus happens practically every time that there will be new bettors for all eventualities and that each of these bettors has a positive mathematical expectation calculated on the basis of his own subjective probabilities. If at a given moment there are certain events E_i for which there are no new bettors, bets on the other events will continue and add to the right-hand member of (8), thus making possible bets on E_i with a positive mathematical expectation. This is what attracts players to pari-mutuel betting; it makes it possible for each one to have a positive mathematical expectation based on his own subjective probabilities, and thus provide him with the certainty of winning in the long run.

It goes without saying that this certainty is illusory even if one ignores the percentage taken by those who operate the pari-mutuel. On the other hand, we cannot say that this conviction of the bettors is always unjustified; for certain well-informed persons having an exceptional flair the subjective probabilities are often very close to what they should be objectively. In fact, the method of pari-mutuel betting, or analogous methods of betting, enable one to assess the merits of the subjective probabilities of a given person after the results have actually been obtained. This is a very interesting problem whose importance goes beyond that of pari-mutuel betting, and we shall say a few more words about it in the next section.

II.7 *The Merits of Subjective Probabilities*

When two persons who consider themselves equally competent assign different subjective probabilities to certain gambles and one can observe them a sufficient number of times, it is often possible to decide which of the two is superior so far as their judgement is concerned.

Let us clarify this statement by means of an example. Suppose that two doctors have observed a certain disease, and on the basis of these observations they have determined the probability that a patient will die from the disease. To be specific, let us say that one of them claims that the probability that a patient will die from the disease within a month (or three months) is 0.30, and that the other claims that the probability is 0.50. The average of these two figures is 0.40, and doctor A who evaluated the probability as 0.30 would judge that it is advantageous to bet $60 to receive $100 if the patient survives. On the other hand, doctor B who evaluated the probability as 0.50 would consider it advantageous to bet 40 dollars to receive $100 if the patient dies. They can thus arrange some sort of pari-mutuel betting scheme; A pays in $60, B pays in $40, and the whole amount will go to A if the patient survives and to B if the patient dies. It could happen, of course, that for some other disease A is more pessimistic than B; in that case A would bet on the patient's dying in the pari-mutuel and B would bet on his recovery.

It is evident that the outcome of a single gamble does not prove anything, or at least not very much. Regardless of whether the probability is 0.30, 0.40, or 0.50, there will be instances where the favorable outcome occurs and there will be instances where it does not occur. There is very little one can conclude from an isolated case like this about the exactness of the evaluation of a probability. However, it is clear that in our example doctor A, who evaluated the probability of a recovery as 0.70, attaches a mathematical expectation of $70 to his bet of $60. On the average he would thus expect to win $10; that is, he would expect to win $1,000 in 100 analogous bets. Hence, if A's gain in 100 such games is about $1,000 (and this gain equals B's loss), one can conclude with a nonnegligible probability that A's estimates are generally superior to those of B. This probability would become a pseudo-certainty if A's gain exceeds $2,000 in 200 bets, and a practically absolute certainty if his gain exceeds $10,000 in 1,000 bets.

Of course, this does not exclude the possibility that at times A's estimates are better than those of B and that at other times they are worse; this cannot be determined by the method we have used. Neither does the method make it possible to judge the absolute merits of A's estimates, for if B's estimates are extremely poor, those of A could be better without actually being very good.

With reference to our medical example, it is difficult to imagine the same patient being examined at one time by a great number of doctors. It is different, however, in horse racing or competitive sports such as tennis or football, where a great number of more or less enlightened amateurs are willing to place bets. In fact, a person who can come out ahead each year at pari-mutuel betting (especially if one accounts for the percentage taken out for administrative expenses) can be certain that his subjective probabilities are closer to the truth than those of the other bettors and, hence, in the large majority of the cases close to the actual objective probabilities.

Nevertheless, this does not mean that this privileged bettor will necessarily win each time; it could happen that he wins very seldom (though each time a large sum), if he is skilful enough to bet on events whose probability is very small, yet greater than it is in the judgment of the other bettors.

Thus, if one has a certain number of bettors whose subjective probabilities seem to be relatively good, the mean of their evaluations may be considered as providing a probability which rightfully can be called objective (especially when their evaluations do not differ very much).

The Petersburg Paradox

III.1 *The Petersburg Paradox*

The problem we shall discuss in this section is the Petersburg paradox, which dates back to the eighteenth century; it has given rise to numerous disputes among eminent specialists in the calculus of probability.

PROBLEM. *Peter and Paul play the game of heads or tails under the following conditions: If Paul wins the first $n - 1$ games and Peter wins the nth, Paul pays Peter 2^n dollars and the game ends. How much should Peter pay Paul to play the game, assuming that the game is to be equitable?*

The answer to this problem is unexpected and improbable, as the name paradox might suggest. The amount Peter must pay is infinite, which means that no matter how much Peter might pay, the game is to his advantage.

We know that Peter's total mathematical expectation is the sum of the mathematical expectations corresponding to the various possibilities. If he wins the nth game (after having lost the first $n - 1$), his gain is 2^n, the probability of this happening is $1/2^n$, and the mathematical expectation is 1. This argument holds regardless of the value of n, which may be as large as desired. Thus, the total mathematical expectation is

$$E = 1 + 1 + 1 + \ldots + 1 + \ldots$$

This series extends indefinitely and E is infinite.

One can give two different answers to this paradox, depending on whether one assumes a concrete or an abstract point of view. Accounting for concrete realities, it is evident that, even with credit, Paul cannot pay a sum exceeding his total fortune; thus, one is forced to modify the conditions in such a way that the game terminates before Paul's possible loss exceeds his total fortune. If this fortune is a billion dollars, they cannot play more than 29 games, since 2^{30} exceeds a billion. The series E would thus end with the 29th term and its value would be 29—not infinity.

Of course, one can also assume the abstract point of view of the mathematician, who can ignore all practical considerations. It does not matter to him that the sum Paul must receive exceeds by far the value of a mass of gold greater in size than the earth or even the sun. It does not matter to him either that if Peter pays Paul not infinity, which is impossible, but a billion dollars each time the game begins, Peter would remain in debt even if he played a game each thousandth of a second for billions of centuries. Of course, if Peter has confidence and perseverance, and if the length of his life is unlimited, the moment will come that an exceptional event will put him ahead.

These are the two solutions to the Petersburg paradox, and everyone may use the one which suits him best. We shall not dwell upon this any longer; instead we shall consider a game suggested by the paradox, which has the appearance of being equitable and which leads to some interesting results.

III.2 *The Petersburg Martingale*

Let us consider two players Peter and Paul who agree to play an equitable game (such as heads or tails) a certain number of times, where the maximum number of games is fixed at n and where Peter has the right to stop the game before the maximum is reached. Furthermore, Peter has the right to fix the stakes, and he fixes them at $(k + 1)2^{k-1}$ for the kth game. Peter will stop playing as soon as he wins a game, in which case his net gain is 2^k when the kth game is the first one he wins. If Peter loses all n games (and only in that case), Paul wins and his winnings will be $n \cdot 2^n$. We shall call this game the Petersburg martingale.

The privileges accorded to Peter do not modify the equitable nature of each game or the whole set of n games, as it can easily be verified that the mathematical expectation is the same for each player. Peter can win in any one of the first n games after having lost all preceding games. In that case his net gain is 2^k if he wins the kth game, the probability that this will happen is $1/2^k$, and the corresponding mathematical expectation is 1; it follows that for the case where Peter wins his total mathematical expectation E is

$$E = 1 + 1 + \ldots + 1 = n$$

since the number of terms equals the maximum number of games.

So far as Paul is concerned, he has a gain only if he wins all n games; the probability that this will happen is $1/2^n$, the gain is $n \cdot 2^n$, and for the case where he wins his mathematical expectation E' is

$$E' = \frac{1}{2^n} \cdot n \cdot 2^n = n$$

The total mathematical expectations of Peter and Paul are thus $E - E'$ and $E' - E$, respectively, and they are both equal to zero. It follows that the game is equitable.

Suppose now that the number of games is not fixed in advance and that Peter has the right to prolong the game as long as he wants. The numbers E and E' will increase indefinitely with n, they will remain equal to each other, and the difference $E - E'$, which is always equal to zero, has zero as its limit. Must one conclude from this that the game remains equitable and that both players' chances of winning remain equal? It is evident that this cannot be the case and that Peter is certain to win; if Peter bets on heads it is impossible that tails will appear indefinitely. Of course, if one assumes a concrete point of view (and not the abstract point of view of the mathematician), it must be regarded as impossible even to obtain tails a billion times in a row (provided there is no trickery). Such a miracle would be as improbable as the miracle of the dactylographic monkeys, although it is nevertheless theoretically possible. However, even for the mathematician who resolves to ignore all real contingencies it is *impossible* for tails to appear *infinitely many times in a row;* according to the rules Paul cannot win if the game terminates and we assumed that it terminates as soon as Peter wins.

It follows that the mathematical expectation E increases indefinitely with n and that it becomes infinite (in the mathematical sense of the term) when n becomes infinite. The same holds for E'. In fact, E' consists of two factors of which one tends to zero while the other increases indefinitely. However, to calculate the *true value* of E' for infinite n one cannot employ the usual methods of algebra on account of the term which becomes zero and which represents a probability.* If this probability is strictly zero, the occurrence of the corresponding event is impossible and the mathematical expectation is zero regardless of the size, or even the infinity, of the possible gain.

If we refer to a sequence of plays ending in a win for Peter as a "series," and if Peter and Paul play many such series, the probability that one of these series is of infinite length is zero, no matter how many series there might be. It would be zero even for a countable infinity of such series.†

If one says that Peter's mathematical expectation is infinite, this means that his average gain increases indefinitely with the number of series played. The growth of this average is fairly slow; it is comparable to the logarithm of the number of series.

---

* In contrast, the reasoning of Section 6.8 concerning mathematical expectations is correct, since the quantities become infinite by addition and not by multiplication.

† This is due to the fact that the power of the continuum exceeds that of a countable set.

Let us recall that all these results were obtained from the point of view of the mathematician, notably that of Joseph Bertrand, that is, by making abstractions. Otherwise one could not visualize series of games whose duration exceeds that of the human life, or payments of amounts corresponding to billions of tons of precious metal. If one considered these practical limitations, one would be led to a fixed maximum stake, a fixed maximum for the number of games in a series, as well as a maximum for the number of series. The probability for Paul to win at least one series would then be small, but not strictly zero. It can thus be seen that the conclusions depend on whether or not this probability is regarded as negligible.

To conclude, we have seen that there are situations where a game does not remain equitable if one plays it an arbitrary number of times or if one plays with arbitrary stakes. The reason it ceases to be equitable is that the number of times it is played is not fixed in advance. In other words, the number of times it is played exceeds any fixed constant, which in fact is the definition of infinity.

If one refuses to visualize infinity, that is, if one takes a concrete point of view, the principle remains purely theoretical. It ceases to be of practical value if the conditions under which Paul wins in this problem have a probability which is so small that one can act as if it equalled zero.

APPENDIX FOUR

IV. 1 *Values of the Function* $\theta(\lambda) = \dfrac{2}{\sqrt{\pi}} \displaystyle\int_0^\lambda e^{-\lambda^2}\, d\lambda$

λ	θ	λ	θ	λ	θ	λ	θ
0.00	0.0000	0.62	0.6194	1.24	0.9205	1.86	0.9915
0.01	0.0113	0.63	0.6270	1.25	0.9229	1.87	0.9918
0.02	0.0226	0.64	0.6346	1.26	0.9252	1.88	0.9922
0.03	0.0339	0.65	0.6420	1.27	0.9275	1.89	0.9925
0.04	0.0451	0.66	0.6494	1.28	0.9297	1.90	0.9928
0.05	0.0564	0.67	0.6566	1.29	0.9319	1.91	0.9931
0.06	0.0676	0.68	0.6638	1.30	0.9340	1.92	0.9934
0.07	0.0789	0.69	0.6708	1.31	0.9361	1.93	0.9937
0.08	0.0901	0.70	0.6778	1.32	0.9381	1.94	0.9939
0.09	0.1013	0.71	0.6847	1.33	0.9400	1.95	0.9942
0.10	0.1125	0.72	0.6914	1.34	0.9419	1.96	0.9944
0.11	0.1236	0.73	0.6981	1.35	0.9438	1.97	0.9947
0.12	0.1348	0.74	0.7047	1.36	0.9457	1.98	0.9949
0.13	0.1459	0.75	0.7112	1.37	0.9473	1.99	0.9951
0.14	0.1569	0.76	0.7175	1.38	0.9490	2.00	0.9953
0.15	0.1680	0.77	0.7238	1.39	0.9507	2.01	0.9955
0.16	0.1790	0.78	0.7300	1.40	0.9523	2.02	0.9957
0.17	0.1900	0.79	0.7361	1.41	0.9538	2.03	0.9959
0.18	0.2009	0.80	0.7421	1.42	0.9554	2.04	0.9961
0.19	0.2118	0.81	0.7480	1.43	0.9569	2.05	0.9963
0.20	0.2227	0.82	0.7538	1.44	0.9583	2.06	0.9964
0.21	0.2335	0.83	0.7595	1.45	0.9597	2.07	0.9966
0.22	0.2443	0.84	0.7651	1.46	0.9611	2.08	0.9967
0.23	0.2550	0.85	0.7707	1.47	0.9624	2.09	0.9969
0.24	0.2657	0.86	0.7761	1.48	0.9637	2.10	0.9970
0.25	0.2763	0.87	0.7814	1.49	0.9649	2.11	0.9972
0.26	0.2869	0.88	0.7867	1.50	0.9661	2.12	0.9973
0.27	0.2974	0.89	0.7918	1.51	0.9673	2.13	0.9974
0.28	0.3079	0.90	0.7969	1.52	0.9684	2.14	0.9975
0.29	0.3183	0.91	0.8019	1.53	0.9695	2.15	0.9976
0.30	0.3286	0.92	0.8068	1.54	0.9706	2.16	0.9977
0.31	0.3389	0.93	0.8116	1.55	0.9716	2.17	0.9979
0.32	0.3491	0.94	0.8163	1.56	0.9726	2.18	0.9980
0.33	0.3593	0.95	0.8209	1.57	0.9736	2.19	0.9980
0.34	0.3694	0.96	0.8254	1.58	0.9745	2.20	0.9981
0.35	0.3794	0.97	0.8299	1.59	0.9755	2.21	0.9982
0.36	0.3893	0.98	0.8342	1.60	0.9763	2.22	0.9983
0.37	0.3992	0.99	0.8385	1.61	0.9772	2.23	0.9984
0.38	0.4090	1.00	0.8427	1.62	0.9780	2.24	0.9985
0.39	0.4187	1.01	0.8468	1.63	0.9788	2.25	0.9985
0.40	0.4284	1.02	0.8508	1.64	0.9796	2.26	0.9986
0.41	0.4380	1.03	0.8548	1.65	0.9804	2.27	0.9987
0.42	0.4475	1.04	0.8686	1.66	0.9811	2.28	0.9987
0.43	0.4569	1.05	0.8624	1.67	0.9818	2.29	0.9988
0.44	0.4662	1.06	0.8661	1.68	0.9825	2.30	0.9989
0.45	0.4755	1.07	0.8698	1.69	0.9832	2.31	0.9989
0.46	0.4847	1.08	0.8733	1.70	0.9838	2.33	0.9990
0.47	0.4937	1.09	0.8768	1.71	0.9844	2.35	0.9991
0.48	0.5027	1.10	0.8802	1.72	0.9850	2.37	0.9992
0.49	0.5117	1.11	0.8835	1.73	0.9856	2.40	0.9993
0.50	0.5205	1.12	0.8868	1.74	0.9861	2.43	0.9994
0.51	0.5292	1.13	0.8900	1.75	0.9867	2.46	0.9995
0.52	0.5379	1.14	0.8931	1.76	0.9872	2.50	0.9996
0.53	0.5465	1.15	0.8961	1.77	0.9877	2.56	0.9997
0.54	0.5549	1.16	0.8991	1.78	0.9882	2.63	0.9998
0.55	0.5633	1.17	0.9020	1.79	0.9886	2.75	0.9999
0.56	0.5716	1.18	0.9048	1.80	0.9891	3.13	0.99999
0.57	0.5798	1.19	0.9076	1.81	0.9895	3.46	0.999999
0.58	0.5879	1.20	0.9103	1.82	0.9899	3.77	0.9999999
0.59	0.5959	1.21	0.9130	1.83	0.9903	4.06	0.99999999
0.60	0.6039	1.22	0.9155	1.84	0.9907	4.34	0.999999999
0.61	0.6117	1.23	0.9181	1.85	0.9911	4.59	0.9999999999
						4.80	0.99999999999

Index